From the Wings of Heaven

Ruby Huffman Hall

THREE SKILLET

FROM THE WINGS OF HEAVEN, Ruby Huffman Hall

1st Ed.

From the Study Notes of Ruby Huffman Hall, a Prayer Warrior and a Mighty Woman of God.

www.ThreeSkilletPublishing.com

Edited by Farley Dunn
Cover Design by Farley Dunn

All Scripture References are from the King James Bible and are found in the Public Domain.

ISBN: 978-1-943189-41-0

— *In Memory* —

Ruby Louise Huffman Hall

1930 to 2016

Contents

Forward

Ruby was a mighty woman of God, a stalwart member of her community, and my mother-in-law. She held nothing in higher esteem than her love of Christ, and she shared that love with everyone she met.

Married to her husband, Edgar, for over 60 years, Ruby lived in the United States, Germany, Turkey, and India. She raised three children, Barbara, David, and Diane, and left numerous grandchildren and great-grandchildren. One of her passions was cooking, and while her children were still teenagers, about 20 Southwest Assembly of God students would regularly join Ruby's family for lunch after Sunday morning services. Cooking for her crowd of "kids" was the highlight of her week.

While raising her family, Ruby never slowed down, working (not always at the same time) as a retail store manager, nursery school teacher, children's counselor, missionary, motivational speaker, in addition to her treasured position of housewife and mother. In her 80s, Ruby moved with her husband, daughter, son-in-law, and grandson to North Carolina. There she discovered the church she described as the light of her life, Park East Church of God. She felt she had found her extended family in Christ. Being asked to serve as a grandparent to the church teens made Ruby feel special, and she loved the youth as her own. She held them up in prayer on a daily basis, telling everyone she met how special they were to her.

While growing up, Ruby's mother teased her that her middle name was "Go." Ruby always wanted to travel. She lived up to her nickname in her 85 years of life on this earth. Over the decades, she visited Hawaii, Alaska, Canada, Mexico, Holland, Austria, Iran, Malaysia, Taiwan, London, and Singapore. Ruby accompanied her family on picnics to the Black Forest of historic Germany, shopped in tropical Singapore, and visited the majestic Taj Mahal in India with her best friend.

In her later years, she and Edgar took a cruise to Alaska with her daughter, Diane, and grandson, Steven. As a treat, Diane and Steven arranged a limousine to ferry Ruby and Edgar around Seattle and to the cruise ship on the day of their departure. Her favorite surprise of the trip was a night in the Radisson Penthouse Suite overlooking the lush green landscape of Seattle, Washington.

On Friday, August 12, 2016, Sister Ruby Hall boarded the ultimate trip with the perfect itinerary. Ruby took her husband's hand and stepped through the veil to stand at Edgar's side in the presence of our Lord. She left on the Chariot of God, riding the ultimate cruise ship to the sky. She journeyed to Heaven in opulent comfort and luxury, and she abides with our Lord and Savior to rest in his arms forevermore.

You'll find Ruby's favorite verses repeatedly cropping up in her study notes. She felt the Blood of Christ and the Joy of the Lord could solve most issues in life, and she was right. She depended on her faith for all her needs, and she now resides at the right hand of the Father.

There's truth in Ruby's collected writings. You'll find her faith, her love of people, and her complete trust in her salvation. Ruby never doubted her Savior's ability to come to her rescue in her time of trouble, and she would be pleased beyond measure to share her collected morsels of faith with you.

Farley Dunn, editor

The Fruit of the Spirit

The orange is an amazing fruit. The peel on the outside covers up what is on the inside. It is the product of the tree, and while the outside provides a beautiful protection, the fruit inside is life-giving.

Proverbs 18:4

> The words of a man's mouth are as deep waters, and the wellspring of wisdom as a flowing brook.

Maturity is a progressive understanding.

Romans 8:11

> But if the Spirit of him that raised up Jesus from the dead dwell in you, he that raised up Christ from the dead shall also quicken your mortal bodies by his Spirit that dwelleth in you.

We are sons of God.

From the Wings of Heaven

/ Notes for a Fulfilling Christian Life \

Galatians 3:26

For ye are all the children of God by faith in Christ Jesus.

I John 4:17

Herein is our love made perfect, that we may have boldness in the day of judgment: because as he is, so are we in this world.

Amos 3:3

Can two walk together, except they be agreed?

You cannot walk with the Lord if you don't agree with him.

Jeremiah 17:7-8

Blessed is the man that trusteth in the Lord, and whose hope the Lord is. For he shall be as a tree planted by the waters, and that spreadeth out her roots by the river, and shall not see when heat cometh, but her leaf shall be green; and shall not be careful in the year of drought, neither shall cease from yielding fruit.

"Blessed is the man that trusteth in the Lord, and whose hope the Lord is. For he shall be as a tree planted by the waters, and that spreadeth out her roots by the river, and shall not see when heat cometh, but her leaf shall be green; and shall not be careful in the year of drought, neither shall cease from yielding fruit."

From the Wings of Heaven

Notes for a Fulfilling Christian Life

Blessed is the man that believes. He shall be like a tree.

Ephesians 5:1-2

> Be ye therefore followers of God, as dear children; And walk in love, as Christ also hath loved us, and hath given himself for us an offering and a sacrifice to God for a sweetsmelling savour.

You will imitate Jesus and watch what you do and say.

Galatians 5:22-23

> But the fruit of the Spirit is love, joy, peace, longsuffering, gentleness, goodness, faith, meekness, temperance: against such there is no law.

1. Love – draws us together in one accord.

2. Joy – gives us a calm delight to leap and spin around with pleasure. It's a present joy and one for the future. It's a *deep, inner joy.* (Psalm 43:3-4; John 16:22; Psalm 5:11; I John 1-4; Proverbs 8:30; John 1:2, 18; Matthew 3:17)

Joy – gives us a calm delight to leap and spin around with pleasure. It's a present joy and one for the future.

3. Peace – is to rest in quietness; to be one with God; Jesus is our Prince of Peace. To be at peace means to be brought into harmony with God. (I Peter 1:2; Isaiah 32:17; II Corinthians 5:17-18; John 14-27)

If you feel unworthy, you don't understand or experience true peace. The peace of God releases the faith of God in you to be able to receive all that God has for you. Rebellion is the opposite of peace.

In Ephesians 2:14, Jesus is our peace.

John 16:33 names Him as a spiritual force.

Isaiah 54:10 says His peace will never be removed.

The peace in our heart is to guide us.

4. Longsuffering – is patience. Psalm 84:10 and James 1:4 remind us to want nothing and not to provoke wrath.

   Hebrews 10:35 and Ephesians 4:2 tell of our lowliness in love and our bond of peace.

   One fruit will blend on into another one.

Gentleness – is softness and strength. Gentleness is never weakness. Make a person feel worthy of what God sees in them. I Thessalonians 2:7-8 says to deal with a person in gentleness.

5. Gentleness – is softness and strength. Gentleness is never weakness. Make a person feel worthy of what God sees in them. I Thessalonians 2:7-8 says to deal with a person in gentleness.

   David said God's gentleness made him great.

6. Goodness – GOD NESS – is good and valuable holiness, made up of all of God's attributes.

   Genesis 1:6 is about the blessing of God.

   Exodus 33:19 tells that all of God's glory passed before him.

   (also Psalm 41; I Peter 3:9; Micah 6:8; Ephesians 5:9; and James 1:17)

7. Meekness – is a gentleness, a teachable spirit. Proverbs 25:15 says it will break down resistance against you. It's a humble heart that doesn't contend with God. Moses was a good example closely linked to humbleness.

Meekness – is a gentleness, a teachable spirit. Proverbs 25:15 says it will break down resistance against you. It's a humble heart that doesn't contend with God. Moses was a good example closely linked to humbleness.

   II Timothy 2:24 says don't fight. Be kind and willing to suffer.

8. Temperance – is strength in self-control. We must crucify self. It's an ability to govern our self by the image of Jesus.

   II Peter 1:6 says to exercise knowledge.

9. Faith – is assurance in whom we believe.

II Peter 1:15 and Romans 1:16-17 says the Bible is the

book of faith.

Galatians 5:22 tells us we will be squeezed, and asks if sweetness or bitterness will come out, like the orange.

Luke 1:75 says we serve Him without fear. We don't have to fear God.

The Cup of the Lord

John 18:11

> Then said Jesus unto Peter, Put up thy sword into the sheath: the cup which my Father hath given me, shall I not drink it?

I Corinthians 11:25

> After the same manner also he took the cup, when he had supped, saying, this cup is the new testament in my blood: this do ye, as oft as ye drink it, in remembrance of me.

1. He partook of the cup of solitude (alone) and loneliness.

He offers us the cup of friendship/fellowship (John 15:15-17).

2. He partook of the cup of bitterness.

He offers us the cup of sweetness.

3. He partook of the cup of betrayal (Matthew 17:22-23).

He offers us the cup of loyalty. He will never leave us or forsake us. A friend closer than a brother. We will never be alone.

4. He partook of the cup of wrath or anger. Everyone was angry with Him, crying, Crucify Him. He felt the wrath of God when He cried, My God, why have you forsaken me? He had to become sin for us.

He offers us the cup of peace.

John 14:27

> Peace I leave with you, my peace I give unto you: not as the world giveth, give I unto you. Let not your heart be troubled, neither let it be afraid.

When we have the kingdom of God within us, we don't have to search for joy. The joy of the Lord is our strength.

By living in the kingdom of God, we have peace within us that the world didn't give and it can't take away.

5. He partook of the cup of bruises – 39 stripes – a horrible cup. Blood ran down. He did it for us.

He offers us the cup of healing. "This is my blood that was given for you." By His stripes, we are healed.

6. He partook of the cup of sorrow. He gave his mother to John to take care of her. It seemed everyone had forsaken Him.

He offers us the cup of joy. When we have the kingdom of God within us, we don't have to search for joy. The joy of the Lord is our strength.

7. He partook of the cup of death. It was a supreme gift. He gave His all. He paid all the penalties of the sins of man. The perfect Lamb was offered as a sacrifice.

He offers us the cup of life.

I John 1:9

> If we confess our sins, he is faithful and just to forgive us our sins, and to cleanse us from all unrighteousness.

Romans 14:17

> For the kingdom of God is not meat and drink; but righteousness, and peace, and joy in the Holy Ghost.

From the Wings of Heaven

Driven by the Spirit

When Adam and Eve fell, they missed out on all the things that God had promised.

It is only through Christ that we are restored.

The angel drove Adam and Eve out from the presence of God. Today, we can either be driven toward God or driven out away from God.

Christ has set forth His Spirit, the driving power of the Holy Ghost, that will keep us pushing on when everything has gone wrong, when everything seems to be falling out of our lives. We must stand on God's Word.

The same Spirit that drove Adam and Eve out of the garden is going to drive us back in. Adam and Eve were severed from the presence of God. Let God push us on to higher and deeper places in Him.

God is looking for a people who will allow the Spirit to drive them on. There is a cry within each of us that is trying to get us to push on and to get to a place that we have never walked before.

God told Moses before he was through with Pharaoh that he would drive Moses and all the people out.

When you start praying, "Mold me and make me the way You want me to be," you are going to be driven by the Spirit. You are going to see things happen in your life. You are going to begin to buck up against some hard places. God is going to allow you to walk through those places where you will begin to focus totally 100% on the Lord your God.

When your friends are pointing a finger at you, saying, this is not God's will, and they are ready to condemn you, walk on with God.

God wants a people who will serve Him completely. Circumstances may not look good, but if you will walk on through them – there is victory ahead.

It may seem that God has led you out, and then you feel you have been made a fool in front of all your friends. When your friends are pointing a finger at you, saying, this is not God's will, and they are ready to condemn you, walk on with God. If you have your peace of God, don't fret about pleasing people. God is right with us in the middle of adversity.

Our eyes are totally on what is in our hand or what is not in our hand. When things begin to fade away, we might say, maybe God's Word doesn't work. Maybe I don't have faith. BUT maybe you are in the will of God. We walk through a lot of things that we wonder why we have to walk through – but we realize later it was for the better. We wouldn't be where we are now if we had not gone through those hard places.

When people begin to come against you and say you must not be right or this wouldn't be happening – that is the time to declare deliverance and claim your blessings.

Job's wife told him to curse God and die.

Sometimes God allows things to get so bad that you have to call on Him. If you could fix it, you wouldn't need Him. But because you need Him, He waits until the very end to prove His power. When we come to those places, we want to sit down. But that is the time to get a new hold on God.

Sometimes God allows things to get so bad that you have to call on Him. If you could fix it, you wouldn't need Him. But because you need Him, He waits until the very end to prove His power.

After Jesus died and was crucified, the disciples were in a room with the door closed, brokenhearted and fearful. In came Jesus through the walls, and He brought a deliverance to them who were afraid. He revealed Himself just when they needed Him most.

Don't give up. Let the Spirit drive you on to victory.

Sometimes we may lose something that is important to us to help us get rid of our pride and keep us humble before Him.

Exodus 6:1

> Then the Lord said unto Moses, Now shalt thou see what I will do to Pharaoh: for with a strong hand shall he let them go, and with a strong hand shall he drive them out of his land.

God speaks to Moses that Pharaoh would drive them out. God raised up Pharaoh that He might show forth His power through him and that "My name might be declared throughout all the earth."

Jesus was baptized in water as a forerunner to our baptism in the Holy Ghost. We become the sons of God. Those that are led by the Spirit of God are the sons of God.

The Spirit drove Jesus into the wilderness to be tempted 40 days, yet the angels ministered to him.

Jesus was baptized in water as a forerunner to our baptism in the Holy Ghost. We become the sons of God. Those that are led by the Spirit of God are the sons of God.

Our comfort zone is upset sometimes. God calls us to prayer and fasting and seeking spiritual things. To whom much is given, much is required. If we love God, we will keep His commandments. The little foxes spoil the vine. The works of the flesh need to come out of us. We need to let the Spirit drive these out of our lives.

If there is a Pharaoh in your life, maybe it is the will of God, that God might show forth His power through that thing you are going through.

God does not send persecutions and trials to perfect us. But sometimes, He allows them to knock at our doors, so that the power of God can be manifested to those that are around you.

As soon as you come into that realm in the Spirit, you can know the enemy will come against you to stop you from seeing God.

Jesus walked in that realm of wilderness and was willing to be driven into the realm of dedication. He came out with power and boldness in the Spirit.

If you don't pray, you won't stay. If you don't fast, you won't last.

It is time to let the Spirit drive us on.

From the Wings of Heaven

Choice – Decision – Consequence

Boston Scientific could have chosen to be just a factory making instruments for the heart with no desire for excellence. Or, they could make the CHOICE to be a quality organization to invest in the most expensive and the best equipment there is to produce the best quality instruments to give us a new lease on life.

Because Boston Scientific made such a marvelous DECISION to give their best in every way, like selecting the most qualified people to work for them, with the most sophisticated equipment, it's a pleasure to tour their campus. Each piece of equipment shown and demonstrated is impressive and awe-inspiring.

The CONSEQUENCES could have been less than quality, and a lot of people could have lost their lives, involving lawsuits. The real consequences are thousands of people being able to live long and quality lives.

Life gives us a CHOICE.

John 15:16

> Ye have not chosen me, but I have chosen you, and ordained you, that ye should go and bring forth fruit, and that your fruit should remain: that whatsoever ye shall ask of the Father in my name, he may give it you.

If any of you lack wisdom, let him ask of God, that giveth to all men liberally.

We must make a DECISION.

James 1:5-8

> If any of you lack wisdom, let him ask of God, that giveth to all men liberally, and upbraideth not; and it shall be given him. But let him ask in faith, nothing wavering. For he that wavereth is like a wave of the sea driven with the wind and tossed. For let not that man think that he shall receive any thing of the Lord. A double minded man is unstable in all his ways.

We live with the CONSEQUENCE.

Philippians 2:9-11

> Wherefore God also hath highly exalted him, and given him a name which is above every name: That at the name of Jesus every knee should bow, of things in heaven, and things in earth, and things under the earth; And that every tongue should confess that Jesus Christ is Lord, to the glory of God the Father.

Peace that Passes All Understanding

Joy – 1) to rejoice; 2) a very glad feeling; 3) happiness; 4) great pleasure; 5) delight

Matthew 25:21, 23

> His lord said unto him, Well done, thou good and faithful servant: thou hast been faithful over a few things, I will make thee ruler over many things: enter thou into the joy of thy lord.

We read of our rewards of faithfulness in these identical verses.

John 3:29

> He that hath the bride is the bridegroom: but the friend of the bridegroom, which standeth and heareth him, rejoiceth greatly because of the bridegroom's

> voice: this my joy therefore is fulfilled.

John's joy was fulfilled at hearing the voice of Jesus.

John 16:22, 24

> And ye now therefore have sorrow: but I will see you again, and your heart shall rejoice, and your joy no man taketh from you.
>
> Hitherto have ye asked nothing in my name: ask, and ye shall receive, that your joy may be full.

We can have a joy that no man can take away. If we ask, our joy can be full.

John 16:20

We can have a joy that no man can take away. If we ask, our joy can be full.

> Verily, verily, I say unto you, That ye shall weep and lament, but the world shall rejoice: and ye shall be sorrowful, but your sorrow shall be turned into joy.

There is sorrow, but in Jesus, there is peace and joy.

Acts 20:22-24

> And now, behold, I go bound in the spirit unto Jerusalem, not knowing the things that shall befall me there: Save that the Holy Ghost witnesseth in every city, saying that bonds and afflictions abide me. But none of these things move me, neither count I my life

> dear unto myself, so that I might finish my course with joy, and the ministry, which I have received of the Lord Jesus, to testify the gospel of the grace of God.

Paul knew what awaited him in Jerusalem, but he was determined to finish his course with joy and the grace of God.

Romans 14:17

> For the kingdom of God is not meat and drink; but righteousness, and peace, and joy in the Holy Ghost.

The kingdom of God is righteousness, peace, and joy.

Hebrews 12:1-2, 11

> Wherefore seeing we also are compassed about with so great a cloud of witnesses, let us lay aside every weight, and the sin which doth so easily beset us, and let us run with patience the race that is set before us, looking unto Jesus the author and finisher of our faith; who for the joy that was set before him endured the cross, despising the shame, and is set down at the right hand of the throne of God.

Paul knew what awaited him in Jerusalem, but he was determined to finish his course with joy and the grace of God.

> Now no chastening for the present seemeth to be joyous, but grievous: nevertheless afterward it yieldeth

> the peaceable fruit of righteousness unto them which are exercised thereby.

Jesus suffered for the joy that was set before Him.

James 1:2 and 1:12

> My brethren, count it all joy when ye fall into divers temptations;
>
> Blessed is the man that endureth temptation: for when he is tried, he shall receive the crown of life, which the Lord hath promised to them that love him.

Jesus suffered for the joy that was set before Him.

We can count it all joy and endure our temptations until we receive our crown of life.

I Peter 4:12

> Beloved, think it not strange concerning the fiery trial which is to try you, as though some strange thing happened unto you:

There are times fiery trials will come against us.

Jude 24

> Now unto him that is able to keep you from falling, and to present you faultless before the presence of his glory with exceeding joy,

Jesus will present us to God with exceeding joy.

John 15:9-12

> As the Father hath loved me, so have I loved you: continue ye in my love. If ye keep my commandments, ye shall abide in my love; even as I have kept my Father's commandments, and abide in his love. These things have I spoken unto you, that my joy might remain in you, and that your joy might be full. This is my commandment, That ye love one another, as I have loved you.

Weeping endureth for the night, but joy cometh in the morning.

Love God and love one another with the same love that your joy might be full.

Psalm 30:5

> For his anger endureth but a moment; in his favour is life: weeping may endure for a night, but joy cometh in the morning.

Weeping endureth for the night, but joy cometh in the morning.

Psalm 16:11

> Thou wilt shew me the path of life: in thy presence is fulness of joy; at thy right hand there are pleasures for evermore.

His presence is full of joy.

Nehemiah 8:10

> Then he said unto them, Go your way, eat the fat, and drink the sweet, and send portions unto them for whom nothing is prepared: for this day is holy unto our Lord: neither be ye sorry; for the joy of the Lord is your strength.

The joy of the Lord is my strength.

Psalm 126:5-6

> They that sow in tears shall reap in joy. He that goeth forth and weepeth, bearing precious seed, shall doubtless come again with rejoicing, bringing his sheaves with him.

If we sow in tears, we will reap in unbounding joy.

If we sow in tears, we will reap in unbounding joy.

Jeremiah 15:16

> Thy words were found, and I did eat them; and thy word was unto me the joy and rejoicing of mine heart: for I am called by thy name, O Lord God of hosts.

Thy words were joy unto me.

God's Word gives us peace that passes all understanding, if we think on Him and stand close to His side.

The Application of the Blood

Theology teaches that Jesus shed His Blood for the sins of the world, and that is all there is to say about it! The danger lies in allowing this to become an historical fact rather than a present, potent reality.

Let's talk about how to apply the Blood. In the natural world, we would have no difficulty understanding how to apply disinfectant to an infection. We would take the disinfectant and sprinkle or pour it upon the infection, and the result would be that all germs and living organisms present in that infection would die.

Now we should have no difficulty in doing the same thing spiritually. Whenever Satan is at work, we must apply the only corrective antidote there is – the Blood of Jesus. There is absolutely no alternative, no substitute. Prayer, praise, worship, and devotion all have their part in our approach to

God; but the Blood of Jesus is the only effective counter-agent to corruption.

This is why Satan has always tried to take the Blood out of our churches. If there is no disinfectant, then his demons are free to continue their deadly work of destruction in spirit, soul, and body.

Having concluded therefore that the Blood of Jesus is our only remedy, how are we to obtain it and use it? In the Old Testament, the priest took a bunch of hyssop and dipped it into the blood and then sprinkled or rough-painted it upon the lintels and door-posts of the houses of the Israelites. But in the spiritual realm, we take of the Blood by faith, and then we SPEAK IT, which is really a form of intercessory prayer. Each time we plead the Blood, we are offering the ONLY PLEA which can bring any results in intercession.

> So the more we plead the Blood, the more power we are bringing to bear against this evil situation.

Think of it this way. The word "Blood" spoken in faith once could be likened to one drop of Blood splashed upon the evil, corruptive situation with which we have to deal in prayer. Obviously, no one putting disinfectant upon corruption at the bottom of a garbage container would use only one drop, would they? So the more we plead the Blood, the more power we are bringing to bear against this evil situation.

But let me warn against mechanical repetition. Obviously, pleading the Blood mechanically in vain repetition is ineffective and foolish, especially to the unbeliever. But for the child of God who pleads the Blood IN FAITH, it quickly brings wonderful results. The whole approach is so simple and obvious to the spiritual mind that we are often amazed that so many people miss it.

In Old Testament times, the priests offered physical sacrifices of animals. The flesh was burned with fire, but the blood was drained into basins and was USED by being sprinkled. Peter tells us that in New Testament times, we are priests who offer spiritual sacrifices acceptable to God by Jesus Christ (I Peter 2:5). Spiritual sacrifices are the New Testament counterparts of the Old Testament physical sacrifices. As New Testament believer-priests, we are to take the living Blood of Jesus and "sprinkle" it with our tongues before the Lord by repeating the word "Blood." Immediately, we begin to bring Satan's work into bondage and nullify his evil workings.

> The blood of Abel spoke vengeance, but the Blood of Jesus carries all the power, spirit, and life that is in Jesus.

The blood of Abel spoke vengeance, but the Blood of Jesus carries all the power, spirit, and life that is in Jesus. As the blood of a human carries life, so does the Blood of Jesus carry the life of the Son of God. Each time we say the word "Blood" in faith, we are bringing the creative lifeforce of the universe to bear upon the destroying power of Satan.

You don't have to continually say the word "Blood" to keep you covered continually. Our Savior and God is with us always.

Faith in Temptation

Evil thoughts will draw us away from God. The devil will give us a strong imagination for things of evil.

1 Corinthians 10:4-5

> And did all drink the same spiritual drink: for they drank of that spiritual Rock that followed them: and that Rock was Christ. But with many of them God was not well pleased: for they were overthrown in the wilderness.

When we delight in our wicked imagination, it becomes lust. We will become enticed, which is the weakening of our will.

1 Corinthians 10:14

> Wherefore, my dearly beloved, flee from idolatry.

Lust is conceived in the yielding to the allure of our imagination.

1 Corinthians 10:15

> I speak as to wise men; judge ye what I say.

Sin is partaking of what we imagine.

Our physical death is the separation of our inner man from our physical one, but spiritual death is when your spirit is alive to Satan. We become eternally dead when we are dead to Christ.

Satan's ultimate goal is to manifest himself in humans. Temptation is a death process. We're not dead at first, but that's where it leads.

Satan's ultimate goal is to manifest himself in humans. Temptation is a death process. We're not dead at first, but that's where it leads.

God's goal in life is to reproduce himself in our human form. He is our healing process, our life, and our overcoming salvation when we're faced with the devil's temptations.

1 Corinthians 10:13

> There hath no temptation taken you but such as is common to man: but God is faithful, who will not suffer you to be tempted above that ye are able; but will with the temptation also make a way to escape, that ye may be able to bear it.

Eight Truths from God

Ask in faith without wavering. If you waver, you won't get anything from God.

If the Word is not working, you don't have enough knowledge. You must be able to stand on the Word.

If you waver when the storm comes, you become part of the destruction.

Our test of humility is a combination of the mind and modesty.

Blessed means having an abundance of favor (pleasure) in the Lord.

Allurement to sin is to be drawn away of your own lust.

God cannot be tempted with evil. If God is in us, we cannot be tempted with evil.

God is single-minded but multi-purposed.

God Is Love

John 3:16

> For God so loved the world, that he gave his only begotten Son, that whosoever believeth in him should not perish, but have everlasting life.

For God so loved the world . . .

John 17:2

> As thou hast given him power over all flesh, that he should give eternal life to as many as thou hast given him.

We are given to Jesus.

John 17:10

> And all mine are thine, and thine are mine; and I am glorified in them.

Jesus is glorified in us.

John 17:20

> Neither pray I for these alone, but for them also which shall believe on me through their word;

This is not only for the disciples, but to all who believe.

John 17:23

> I in them, and thou in me, that they may be made perfect in one; and that the world may know that thou hast sent me, and hast loved them, as thou hast loved me.

God loves us as he loved Jesus.

John 17:26

> And I have declared unto them thy name, and will declare it: that the love wherewith thou hast loved me may be in them, and I in them.

The love that is in Jesus is in us. We have been chosen by God as a gift to be given to Jesus (for his bride). Like Abraham sent the servant to find a bride for Isaac, they both loved each other and God blessed their lives together.

The love that is in Jesus is in us. We have been chosen by God as a gift to be given to Jesus (for his bride). Like Abraham sent the servant to find a bride for Isaac, they both loved each other and God blessed their lives together.

Samson sought after his own bride and ran into all kinds of trouble, even to the point of losing his life.

We are the bride of Christ. We have been chosen of God by the Holy Spirit to be the bride of Christ, to be given the same love that God has given Christ.

Sometimes the enemy (Satan) comes against us. He hates Jesus, and since he has already been defeated by the power of Jesus, he tries to hurt Him by attacking His bride. In life, sometimes if a girl gets mad at her girlfriend, she will strike back at her by trying to take her boyfriend. Even if she doesn't really care for him, it is a way of hurting the other girl.

Sometimes the enemy (Satan) comes against us. He hates Jesus, and since he has already been defeated by the power of Jesus, he tries to hurt Him by attacking His bride.

John 17:2, 6

> As thou hast given him power over all flesh, that he should give eternal life to as many as thou hast given him. I have manifested thy name unto the men which thou gavest me out of the world: thine they were, and thou gavest them me; and they have kept thy word.

God has given us to Jesus for His bride. Like in weddings, the minister says, "Who gives this woman?" The father says, "I do." So the heavenly Father gives us to Jesus for His bride.

In the spirit, the more we love the bridegroom, the more we love each other. Not so in the natural. If a girl loves a guy, she doesn't want others loving him.

Revelation 21:2, 9

> And I John saw the holy city, new Jerusalem, coming down from God out of heaven, prepared as a bride adorned for her husband.
>
> And there came unto me one of the seven angels which had the seven vials full of the seven last plagues, and talked with me, saying, Come hither, I will shew thee the bride, the Lamb's wife.

The Spirit and the bride say come.

Revelation 22:17

> And the Spirit and the bride say, Come. And let him that heareth say, Come. And let him that is athirst come. And whosoever will, let him take the water of life freely.

The Spirit and the bride say come.

Ephesians 5:25-27

> Husbands, love your wives, even as Christ also loved the church, and gave himself for it; that he might sanctify and cleanse it with the washing of water by

> the word, that he might present it to himself a glorious church, not having spot, or wrinkle, or any such thing; but that it should be holy and without blemish.

We must be without spot or wrinkle.

John 15:9-13

> As the Father hath loved me, so have I loved you: continue ye in my love. If ye keep my commandments, ye shall abide in my love; even as I have kept my Father's commandments, and abide in his love. These things have I spoken unto you, that my joy might remain in you, and that your joy might be full. This is my commandment, That ye love one another, as I have loved you. Greater love hath no man than this, that a man lay down his life for his friends.

What manner of love is this that He should die for us?

Greater love hath no man . . .

1 John 3:1-5

> Behold, what manner of love the Father hath bestowed upon us, that we should be called the sons of God: therefore the world knoweth us not, because it knew him not. Beloved, now are we the sons of God, and it doth not yet appear what we shall be: but we know that, when he shall appear, we shall be like

> him; for we shall see him as he is.
>
> And every man that hath this hope in him purifieth himself, even as he is pure. Whosoever committeth sin transgresseth also the law: for sin is the transgression of the law. And ye know that he was manifested to take away our sins; and in him is no sin.

What manner of love is this that He should die for us?

The Power of Christ

Plead – to present a statement.

Psalm 35:1

> Plead my cause, O Lord, with them that strive with me: fight against them that fight against me.

Psalm 43:1

> Judge me, O God, and plead my cause against an ungodly nation: O deliver me from the deceitful and unjust man.

Psalm 119:54

> Thy statutes have been my songs in the house of my pilgrimage.

Hebrews 12:24

> And to Jesus the mediator of the new covenant, and

> to the blood of sprinkling, that speaketh better things than that of Abel.

Luke 22:39, 42

> And he came out, and went, as he was wont, to the mount of Olives; and his disciples also followed him. Saying, Father, if thou be willing, remove this cup from me: nevertheless not my will, but thine, be done.

He shed His Blood on the ground. There is power in your will; Christ will empower you to do good.

We have a will, but it takes the power of the Blood to be able to do His will.

Romans 7:14

> For we know that the law is spiritual: but I am carnal, sold under sin.

We have a will, but it takes the power of the Blood to be able to do His will.

Everyone has a right to choose, but everyone doesn't have the power to do as he chooses.

Luke 22:42

> Saying, Father, if thou be willing, remove this cup from me: nevertheless not my will, but thine, be done.

Not our will, but God's will be done. The sins of the flesh

bleed into our lives if we don't take care of them.

Ezekiel 33:26

> Ye stand upon your sword, ye work abomination, and ye defile every one his neighbour's wife: and shall ye possess the land?

Put within you a new heart, and know that God is your salvation.

How to Plead the Blood

The year was 1908-1909. The place was Great Britain. Many independent Assemblies sprang up. Since they weren't under any legislative organizations, they could let the Spirit of God lead them. There were no limitations on them.

Many believers, so recently baptized in the Spirit, with the Shekinah resting upon them, used to plead the Blood of Jesus in strong repetition for all that burdened their hearts: unsaved relatives, troubles in the home, or troubles in the nation. Realizing they had *access into the throne room of God,* they went in boldly with the Blood of Jesus, under the baptism in the Holy Ghost. The Blood of Jesus was a very powerful weapon against evil spirits that would oppose answer to prayer.

Daniel battled it out for three weeks while Michael and Gabriel battled it out in the spirit. The pleading of the Blood will help us in battles with unseen demonic forces to get answers to our prayers.

When one begins to plead the Blood out loud, it will cause others to oppose. The power of the Blood of Jesus will break barriers and set the captives free.

Since the life of God is in the Blood, if we plead, honor, sprinkle, and sing about the Blood, we are actually introducing the life of the Godhead into our worship. Our prayers and requests become charged with the life and power of Jesus. No wonder Satan will do all he can to suppress any teaching on the Blood. He hates it more than anything.

> When the pleading of the Blood was first practiced, there was no teaching on it. The practice commenced spontaneously under the strong, impulsive power of the Holy Ghost.

Unbelievers will use the name of Jesus, but never do you hear them speak of the Blood.

We can receive nothing from God apart from His mercy and Jesus' shed Blood.

Revelations 1:6

> And hath made us kings and priests unto God and his Father; to him be glory and dominion for ever and ever. Amen.

We are kings and priests, and we can enter in whenever we desire. There is no waiting list, but we must enter in with his Blood.

When the pleading of the Blood was first practiced, there was no teaching on it. The practice commenced spontaneously under the strong, impulsive power of the Holy Ghost. God desired to manifest His power, but it could only come forth as the Blood was honored, for His life is in the Blood.

Romans 3:25

> Whom God hath set forth to be a propitiation through faith in his blood, to declare his righteousness for the remission of sins that are past, through the forbearance of God;

To plead the Blood without faith, or with our hearts full of fear, is both repulsive and ineffectual. When we plead the Blood audibly, care should always be taken to do so in simple believing faith; then it will prevail.

> We, the New Testament sons of the High Priest Jesus, may now sprinkle Blood for forgiveness, salvation, redemption, healing, protection, and victory.

The Israelites sprinkled blood in Egypt, and it brought deliverance.

Rahab used the blood-line token, and it brought deliverance.

The High Priests of the Old Testament sprinkled blood, and it brought forgiveness.

Jesus sprinkled His Own Blood and purchased salvation for all mankind!!

We, the New Testament sons of the High Priest Jesus, may now sprinkle Blood for forgiveness, salvation, redemption, healing, protection, and victory.

Exodus 12:24

> And ye shall observe this thing (the sprinkling of the Blood) for an ordinance to thee and to thy sons for ever.

If the Blood is to be sprinkled today, then it must be the New Testament priests who do it – and we are those priests if we believe in the Son of God.

Set Apart

Frontlets or phylacteries are strips of parchments written with four passages of scriptures in ink prepared for the purpose.

They were rolled up in a case of black calf skin which was attached to a stiffer piece of leather, having a thong one finger broad and one-and-a-half cubits long. They were placed at the bend of the arm (left). Those worn on the forehead were written on four strips of parchment and put into four little cells with a square case.

The men wore these at prayer times, usually in the morning and evening.

Exodus 13:1-10

> And the Lord spake unto Moses, saying, Sanctify unto me all the firstborn, whatsoever openeth the womb among the children of Israel, both of man and

of beast: it is mine.

And Moses said unto the people, Remember this day, in which ye came out from Egypt, out of the house of bondage; for by strength of hand the Lord brought you out from this place: there shall no leavened bread be eaten. This day came ye out in the month Abib. And it shall be when the Lord shall bring thee into the land of the Canaanites, and the Hittites, and the Amorites, and the Hivites, and the Jebusites, which he sware unto thy fathers to give thee, a land flowing with milk and honey, that thou shalt keep this service in this month.

> Remember the day you came out of bondage. Tell your children. Keep this from year to year.

Seven days thou shalt eat unleavened bread, and in the seventh day shall be a feast to the Lord. Unleavened bread shall be eaten seven days; and there shall no leavened bread be seen with thee, neither shall there be leaven seen with thee in all thy quarters. And thou shalt shew thy son in that day, saying, This is done because of that which the Lord did unto me when I came forth out of Egypt.

And it shall be for a sign unto thee upon thine hand, and for a memorial between thine eyes, that the Lord's law may be in thy mouth: for with a strong hand hath the Lord brought thee out of Egypt. Thou shalt therefore keep this ordinance in his season from year to year.

Remember the day you came out of bondage. For seven days, eat unleavened bread, and on the seventh day, have a feast of the Lord. Tell your children. Keep this from year to year.

Exodus 13:11-16

> And it shall be when the Lord shall bring thee into the land of the Canaanites, as he sware unto thee and to thy fathers, and shall give it thee, that thou shalt set apart unto the Lord all that openeth the matrix, and every firstling that cometh of a beast which thou hast; the males shall be the Lord's. And every firstling of an ass thou shalt redeem with a lamb; and if thou wilt not redeem it, then thou shalt break his neck: and all the firstborn of man among thy children shalt thou redeem.

The first born should be set apart unto the Lord as a sign that all the first born were saved. Tell this to your children.

> And it shall be when thy son asketh thee in time to come, saying, What is this? that thou shalt say unto him, By strength of hand the Lord brought us out from Egypt, from the house of bondage: And it came to pass, when Pharaoh would hardly let us go, that the Lord slew all the firstborn in the land of Egypt, both the firstborn of man, and the firstborn of beast:

> therefore I sacrifice to the Lord all that openeth the matrix, being males; but all the firstborn of my children I redeem. And it shall be for a token upon thine hand, and for frontlets between thine eyes: for by strength of hand the Lord brought us forth out of Egypt.

The first born should be set apart unto the Lord as a sign that all the first born were saved. Tell this to your children.

Deuteronomy 6:4-9

> Hear, O Israel: The Lord our God is one Lord: And thou shalt love the Lord thy God with all thine heart, and with all thy soul, and with all thy might. And these words, which I command thee this day, shall be in thine heart:
>
> And thou shalt teach them diligently unto thy children, and shalt talk of them when thou sittest in thine house, and when thou walkest by the way, and when thou liest down, and when thou risest up. And thou shalt bind them for a sign upon thine hand, and they shall be as frontlets between thine eyes. And thou shalt write them upon the posts of thy house,

"And thou shalt teach them diligently unto thy children, and shalt talk of them when thou sittest in thine house, and when thou walkest by the way, and when thou liest down, and when thou risest up."

and on thy gates.

Deuteronomy 11:13-21

And it shall come to pass, if ye shall hearken diligently unto my commandments which I command you this day, to love the Lord your God, and to serve him with all your heart and with all your soul, that I will give you the rain of your land in his due season, the first rain and the latter rain, that thou mayest gather in thy corn, and thy wine, and thine oil. And I will send grass in thy fields for thy cattle, that thou mayest eat and be full.

"Take heed to yourselves, that your heart be not deceived, and ye turn aside, and serve other gods, and worship them."

Take heed to yourselves, that your heart be not deceived, and ye turn aside, and serve other gods, and worship them; And then the Lord's wrath be kindled against you, and he shut up the heaven, that there be no rain, and that the land yield not her fruit; and lest ye perish quickly from off the good land which the Lord giveth you.

Therefore shall ye lay up these my words in your heart and in your soul, and bind them for a sign upon your hand, that they may be as frontlets between your eyes. And ye shall teach them your children, speaking of them when thou sittest in thine house, and

> when thou walkest by the way, when thou liest down, and when thou risest up. And thou shalt write them upon the door posts of thine house, and upon thy gates: That your days may be multiplied, and the days of your children, in the land which the Lord sware unto your fathers to give them, as the days of heaven upon the earth.

We celebrate Thanksgiving each year. It is set apart for us to give thanks unto God.

Our Coming Joy

There does come a joy known to those who suffer with Me. But that is not the result of the suffering, but the result of the close intimacy with Me, to which suffering drove you.

I Peter 4:12-13

> Beloved, think it not strange concerning the fiery trial which is to try you, as though some strange thing happened unto you: But rejoice, inasmuch as ye are partakers of Christ's sufferings; that, when his glory shall be revealed, ye may be glad also with exceeding joy.

Daniel 3:17-18, 24-25

> If it be so, our God whom we serve is able to deliver us from the burning fiery furnace, and he will deliver us out of thine hand, O king. But if not, be it known unto thee, O king, that we will not serve thy gods, nor

worship the golden image which thou hast set up.

Then Nebuchadnezzar the king was astonished, and rose up in haste, and spake, and said unto his counsellors, Did not we cast three men bound into the midst of the fire? They answered and said unto the king, True, O king. He answered and said, Lo, I see four men loose, walking in the midst of the fire, and they have no hurt; and the form of the fourth is like the Son of God.

The three Hebrew children found themselves in the fiery furnace knowing their God would deliver them. Jesus appeared in the midst of them.

The three Hebrew children found themselves in the fiery furnace knowing their God would deliver them. Jesus appeared in the midst of them.

The disciples fished all night and were weary. Jesus came and told them to cast their net on the other side. Then when they came to shore, He had fish already cooked for them. He appeared and met their need.

John 21:1-12

After these things Jesus shewed himself again to the disciples at the sea of Tiberias; and on this wise shewed he himself. There were together Simon Peter, and Thomas called Didymus, and Nathanael of Cana in Galilee, and the sons of Zebedee, and two other of his disciples. Simon Peter saith unto them, I go a fishing. They say unto him, We also go with thee. They went forth, and entered into a ship immediately; and that night they caught nothing.

But when the morning was now come, Jesus stood on the shore: but the disciples knew not that it was Jesus. Then Jesus saith unto them, Children, have ye any meat? They answered him, No. And he said unto them, Cast the net on the right side of the ship, and ye shall find. They cast therefore, and now they were not able to draw it for the multitude of fishes. Therefore that disciple whom Jesus loved saith unto Peter, It is the Lord. Now when Simon Peter heard that it was the Lord, he girt his fisher's coat unto him, (for he was naked,) and did cast himself into the sea.

> "Jesus stood on the shore: but the disciples knew not that it was Jesus. Then Jesus saith unto them, Children, have ye any meat? They answered him, No. And he said unto them, Cast the net on the right side of the ship, and ye shall find."

And the other disciples came in a little ship; (for they were not far from land, but as it were two hundred cubits,) dragging the net with fishes. As soon then as they were come to land, they saw a fire of coals there, and fish laid thereon, and bread.

Jesus saith unto them, Bring of the fish which ye have now caught. Simon Peter went up, and drew the net to land full of great fishes, an hundred and fifty and three: and for all there were so many, yet was not the net broken. Jesus saith unto them, Come and dine. And none of the disciples durst ask him, Who art thou? knowing that it was the Lord.

Jonah was in the belly of the whale because of his disobedience. But, still, when he called on God, He delivered him.

Jonah was in the belly of the whale because of his disobedience. But, still, when he called on God, He delivered him.

John 20:19-23

Then the same day at evening, being the first day of the week, when the doors were shut where the disciples were assembled for fear of the Jews, came Jesus and stood in the midst, and saith unto them, Peace be unto you. And when he had so said, he shewed unto them his hands and his side. Then were the disciples glad, when they saw the Lord.

Then said Jesus to them again, Peace be unto you: as my Father hath sent me, even so send I you. And when he had said this, he breathed on them, and saith unto them, Receive ye the Holy Ghost: Whose soever

> sins ye remit, they are remitted unto them; and whose soever sins ye retain, they are retained.

The disciples were behind locked doors, with fear and trembling and broken hearts. Jesus broke all barriers and came to them, saying, Peace be unto you.

JESUS' POWER (THE SPIRIT OF GOD) WILL BREAK ALL BARRIERS TO COME TO OUR RESCUE!!!

The Sacrifice of Christ

Exodus 12:23

> For the Lord will pass through to smite the Egyptians; and when he seeth the blood upon the lintel, and on the two side posts, the Lord will pass over the door, and will not suffer the destroyer to come in unto your houses to smite you.

God says, "When I see the blood, I will pass over you."

Atonement – a) the redemptive life and death of Christ; b) the reconciliation of God and man, thus brought about by Christ

Isiah 53:2

> For he shall grow up before him as a tender plant, and as a root out of a dry ground: he hath no form nor comeliness; and when we shall see him, there is

no beauty that we should desire him.

Jesus had no beauty that we should desire Him. He was stripped of His outward covering. He was covered with His Own Blood. In turn, we may cover our nakedness with His Precious Blood – a perfect atonement or covering, indeed! We must come to Him as naked and destitute of all covering in His presence. Then He will give us His own blessed robe of righteousness after we have accepted the cleansing of His Precious Blood.

Atonement – a) the redemptive life and death of Christ; b) the reconciliation of God and man, thus brought about by Christ

Leviticus 17:11

For the life of the flesh is in the blood: and I have given it to you upon the altar to make an atonement for your souls: for it is the blood that maketh an atonement for the soul.

I John 5:8

And there are three that bear witness in earth, the Spirit, and the water, and the blood: and these three agree in one.

Ephesians 5:26

That he might sanctify and cleanse it with the washing of water by the word,

The Word without the Blood is ineffectual, for the life of Jesus is in the Blood.

> Had Isaac not been spared, there would not have been an Israel, for Isaac was Abraham's only son. So Isaac was a miraculously delivered child, saved by blood.

This is why we partake of communion. When we honor the Blood, the Holy Spirit immediately manifests His life on our behalf.

The book in the Old Testament was sprinkled with blood. Jesus on the cross, *Living Word,* was sprinkled with His Own Blood *Atonement.*

Abraham offered a ram provided by God as a sacrifice instead of Isaac. Had Isaac not been spared, there would not have been an Israel, for Isaac was Abraham's only son. So Isaac was a miraculously delivered child, *saved by blood.* Every Israelite was taught this story and understood the value of the blood.

Exodus 12:22-27

> And ye shall take a bunch of hyssop, and dip it in the blood that is in the bason, and strike the lintel and the two side posts with the blood that is in the bason; and none of you shall go out at the door of his house until the morning. For the Lord will pass through to smite

> the Egyptians; and when he seeth the blood upon the lintel, and on the two side posts, the Lord will pass over the door, and will not suffer the destroyer to come in unto your houses to smite you. And ye shall observe this thing for an ordinance to thee and to thy sons for ever.
>
> And it shall come to pass, when ye be come to the land which the Lord will give you, according as he hath promised, that ye shall keep this service. And it shall come to pass, when your children shall say unto you, What mean ye by this service? That ye shall say, It is the sacrifice of the Lord's passover, who passed over the houses of the children of Israel in Egypt, when he smote the Egyptians, and delivered our houses. And the people bowed the head and worshipped.

God will not suffer the destroyer to come in unto your houses to destroy you, if you have the blood on your doorpost. It must be put there by the household.

God will not suffer the destroyer to come in unto your houses to destroy you, if you have the blood on your doorpost. It must be put there by the household.

In Joshua we read about Rahab and the scarlet thread.

Exodus 12:13

> And the blood shall be to you for a token upon the houses where ye are: and when I see the blood, I will pass over you, and the plague shall not be upon you to destroy you, when I smite the land of Egypt.

Jesus has no appeal to the worldly-wise and self-righteous. He came to those who need a physician.

Revelation 13:8

> And all that dwell upon the earth shall worship him, whose names are not written in the book of life of the Lamb slain from the foundation of the world.

The Blood of Jesus as a redemption for sin was in the mind of the Father from the very beginning of time.

Joshua 2:21

> And she said, According unto your words, so be it. And she sent them away, and they departed: and she bound the scarlet line in the window.

According to thy words, be it so. Yes, there is a Blood line, and the great destroyer cannot get through it; but you must put it there.

According to thy words, be it so. Yes, there is a Blood line, and the great destroyer cannot get through it; but you must put it there. Rahab's household was saved. God is concerned about whole families. Rahab became a part of Israel – like we are today – by faith.

Even before this, when the High Priest was ordained to the priesthood, part of his ordination included putting blood upon:

1. the tip of his right ear so that blood will cleanse all that enters his ears
2. the thumb of his right hand, so that everything that he puts his hand to is cleansed
3. the big toe of his right foot, so that wherever he walks will be cleansed

Rahab's household was saved. God is concerned about whole families. Rahab became a part of Israel – like we are today – by faith.

The Blood of Jesus will keep Satan away from our thought life, our work life, and wherever we go.

Hebrews 10:16-23

> This is the covenant that I will make with them after those days, saith the Lord, I will put my laws into their hearts, and in their minds will I write them; and their sins and iniquities will I remember no more. Now where remission of these is, there is no more offering for sin. Having therefore, brethren, boldness

to enter into the holiest by the blood of Jesus, by a new and living way, which he hath consecrated for us, through the veil, that is to say, his flesh; and having an high priest over the house of God; let us draw near with a true heart in full assurance of faith, having our hearts sprinkled from an evil conscience, and our bodies washed with pure water. Let us hold fast the profession of our faith without wavering; (for he is faithful that promised;)

> To plead the Blood of Jesus is to confess to God that we are depending wholly on His mercy. When we plead the Blood of Jesus, it immediately pleads for us, because it is a SPEAKING BLOOD.

Hebrews 12:24

And to Jesus the mediator of the new covenant, and to the blood of sprinkling, that speaketh better things than that of Abel.

Genesis 4:9-10

And the Lord said unto Cain, Where is Abel thy brother? And he said, I know not: Am I my brother's keeper? And he said, What hast thou done? the voice of thy brother's blood crieth unto me from the ground.

Abel's blood cried vengeance, but Jesus' blood cries mercy.

To plead the Blood of Jesus is to confess to God that we are depending wholly on His mercy. When we plead the Blood of Jesus, it immediately pleads for us, because it is a SPEAKING BLOOD. It speaks mercy from the mercy seat in Heaven where Jesus is seated with His Father.

To those who have discovered this secret, the whole realm of God's power is opened, and all the angels in Heaven come to help and rescue the child of God who honors, uses, and pleads the Blood of Jesus. The Spirit answers to the Blood.

We should use the Blood of Jesus as a covering.

I Peter 2:5

> Ye also, as lively stones, are built up a spiritual house, an holy priesthood, to offer up spiritual sacrifices, acceptable to God by Jesus Christ.

We are as the priest who offered up the blood sacrifices on behalf of the people. We offer the Blood of Jesus as our plea on behalf of ourselves, our children, and our loved ones.

We are as the priest who offered up the blood sacrifices on behalf of the people. We offer the Blood of Jesus as our plea on behalf of ourselves, our children, and our loved ones.

The destroyer gets through the Blood line only one way, if it has been let down – *by disobedience.*

The Joy Set Before Us

Just because you have grief or sorrow, you are not out of the flow of the Holy Ghost. The same Spirit that moved Jesus will move us, if we know the full flow of the Spirit.

John 16:19-33

> Now Jesus knew that they were desirous to ask him, and said unto them, Do ye enquire among yourselves of that I said, A little while, and ye shall not see me: and again, a little while, and ye shall see me? Verily, verily, I say unto you, That ye shall weep and lament, but the world shall rejoice: and ye shall be sorrowful, but your sorrow shall be turned into joy. A woman when she is in travail hath sorrow, because her hour is come: but as soon as she is delivered of the child, she remembereth no more the anguish, for joy that a man is born into the world.
>
> And ye now therefore have sorrow: but I will see you

again, and your heart shall rejoice, and your joy no man taketh from you. And in that day ye shall ask me nothing. Verily, verily, I say unto you, Whatsoever ye shall ask the Father in my name, he will give it you. Hitherto have ye asked nothing in my name: ask, and ye shall receive, that your joy may be full. These things have I spoken unto you in proverbs: but the time cometh, when I shall no more speak unto you in proverbs, but I shall shew you plainly of the Father.

> We read of the woman in travail, revealing the sorrow for Jesus leaving. Yet, Jesus says, in Him they would have peace in the world and through their tribulation.

At that day ye shall ask in my name: and I say not unto you, that I will pray the Father for you: For the Father himself loveth you, because ye have loved me, and have believed that I came out from God. I came forth from the Father, and am come into the world: again, I leave the world, and go to the Father. His disciples said unto him, Lo, now speakest thou plainly, and speakest no proverb. Now are we sure that thou knowest all things, and needest not that any man should ask thee: by this we believe that thou camest forth from God.

Jesus answered them, Do ye now believe? Behold,

> the hour cometh, yea, is now come, that ye shall be scattered, every man to his own, and shall leave me alone: and yet I am not alone, because the Father is with me. These things I have spoken unto you, that in me ye might have peace. In the world ye shall have tribulation: but be of good cheer; I have overcome the world.

We build ourselves up and keep ourselves in love. Christ is able to keep us and give us exceeding joy.

We read of the woman in travail, revealing the sorrow for Jesus leaving. Yet, Jesus says, in Him they would have peace in the world and through their tribulation.

Jude 17-25

> But, beloved, remember ye the words which were spoken before of the apostles of our Lord Jesus Christ; how that they told you there should be mockers in the last time, who should walk after their own ungodly lusts. These be they who separate themselves, sensual, having not the Spirit.
>
> But ye, beloved, building up yourselves on your most holy faith, praying in the Holy Ghost, keep yourselves in the love of God, looking for the mercy of our Lord Jesus Christ unto eternal life. And of some have compassion, making a difference: And others

> save with fear, pulling them out of the fire; hating even the garment spotted by the flesh.
>
> Now unto him that is able to keep you from falling, and to present you faultless before the presence of his glory with exceeding joy, to the only wise God our Saviour, be glory and majesty, dominion and power, both now and ever. Amen.

We build ourselves up and keep ourselves in love. Christ is able to keep us and give us exceeding joy.

Acts 20:22-24

> And now, behold, I go bound in the spirit unto Jerusalem, not knowing the things that shall befall me there: Save that the Holy Ghost witnesseth in every city, saying that bonds and afflictions abide me. But none of these things move me, neither count I my life dear unto myself, so that I might finish my course with joy, and the ministry, which I have received of the Lord Jesus, to testify the gospel of the grace of God.

Paul knew what awaited him in Jerusalem, but he was determined to finish his course with joy.

Paul knew what awaited him in Jerusalem, but he was determined to finish his course with joy.

II Timothy 4:6-8

> For I am now ready to be offered, and the time of my

> departure is at hand. I have fought a good fight, I have finished my course, I have kept the faith: Henceforth there is laid up for me a crown of righteousness, which the Lord, the righteous judge, shall give me at that day: and not to me only, but unto all them also that love his appearing.

Paul fought a good fight, and a crown of joy was laid up for him.

Paul fought a good fight, and a crown of joy was laid up for him.

James 1:2-4

> My brethren, count it all joy when ye fall into divers temptations; Knowing this, that the trying of your faith worketh patience. But let patience have her perfect work, that ye may be perfect and entire, wanting nothing.

Count it all joy in temptation.

James 1:12

> Blessed is the man that endureth temptation: for when he is tried, he shall receive the crown of life, which the Lord hath promised to them that love him.

Blessed is the man that endureth temptation, for he will receive a crown of life.

1 Peter 4:12-13

> Beloved, think it not strange concerning the fiery

> trial which is to try you, as though some strange thing happened unto you: But rejoice, inasmuch as ye are partakers of Christ's sufferings; that, when his glory shall be revealed, ye may be glad also with exceeding joy.

We'll have fiery trials to try our faith.

> Our weeping will endure for the night, but we'll receive joy in the morning.

Psalm 30:5

> For his anger endureth but a moment; in his favour is life: weeping may endure for a night, but joy cometh in the morning.

Our weeping will endure for the night, but we'll receive joy in the morning.

Psalm 16:11

> Thou wilt shew me the path of life: in thy presence is fulness of joy; at thy right hand there are pleasures for evermore.

In His presence is fullness of joy. At His right hand, there are pleasures forever more.

Nehemiah 8:10

> Then he said unto them, Go your way, eat the fat, and drink the sweet, and send portions unto them for whom nothing is prepared: for this day is holy unto

> our Lord: neither be ye sorry; for the joy of the Lord is your strength.

The joy of the Lord is your strength.

Psalm 126:5-6

> They that sow in tears shall reap in joy. He that goeth forth and weepeth, bearing precious seed, shall doubtless come again with rejoicing, bringing his sheaves with him.

Joy has little to do with big smiles and laughter. The Hebrew children were in the fiery furnace, but Jesus was with them in the midst of the tribulation, and they were surrounded with the joy of the Lord.

What we sow in tears, we will reap in joy.

Joy has little to do with big smiles and laughter. The Hebrew children were in the fiery furnace, but Jesus was with them in the midst of the tribulation, and they were surrounded with the joy of the Lord.

Hebrews 12:1-2

> Wherefore seeing we also are compassed about with so great a cloud of witnesses, let us lay aside every weight, and the sin which doth so easily beset us, and let us run with patience the race that is set before us, looking unto Jesus the author and finisher of our faith; who for the

> joy that was set before him endured the cross, despising the shame, and is set down at the right hand of the throne of God.

Jesus endured the cross, despising the shame, for the joy that was set before him. Jesus knew down through the ages we believers would bring joy to Him through worship (Hebrews 16:21).

John 15:9-17

> As the Father hath loved me, so have I loved you: continue ye in my love. If ye keep my commandments, ye shall abide in my love; even as I have kept my Father's commandments, and abide in his love. These things have I spoken unto you, that my joy might remain in you, and that your joy might be full.

Jesus endured the cross, despising the shame, for the joy that was set before him.

> This is my commandment, That ye love one another, as I have loved you. Greater love hath no man than this, that a man lay down his life for his friends. Ye are my friends, if ye do whatsoever I command you.

> Henceforth I call you not servants; for the servant knoweth not what his lord doeth: but I have called you friends; for all things that I have heard of my Fa-

> ther I have made known unto you. Ye have not chosen me, but I have chosen you, and ordained you, that ye should go and bring forth fruit, and that your fruit should remain: that whatsoever ye shall ask of the Father in my name, he may give it you. These things I command you, that ye love one another.

Keep His commandments. Abide in His love and be filled with His joy.

John 3:29

> He that hath the bride is the bridegroom: but the friend of the bridegroom, which standeth and heareth him, rejoiceth greatly because of the bridegroom's voice: this my joy therefore is fulfilled.

John had heard the voice of the bridegroom (Jesus). We are the bride of Christ.

Sin brings great agony, but your sorrow will be turned into joy, which no man can take from you. Sin brought women the travail with child, but when it is brought forth, the joy of the birth washes away all the remembrance of the

Sin brings great agony, but your sorrow will be turned into joy, which no man can take from you. Sin brought women the travail with child, but when it is brought forth, the joy of the birth washes away all the remembrance of the travail. It evaporates.

travail. It evaporates. This body is the source of all corruption, and we long to be delivered from this struggle.

It is the joy that is set before us – that we endure our temptation in Christ.

Acid and Gold

Luke 22:31

> And the Lord said, Simon, Simon, behold, Satan hath desired to have you, that he may sift you as wheat:

Satan hath desired to have you, that he may sift you as wheat: but I have prayed for thee, that thy faith fail not: and when thou are converted, strengthen thy brethren.

I Corinthians 10:12-13

> Wherefore let him that thinketh he standeth take heed lest he fall. There hath no temptation taken you but such as is common to man: but God is faithful, who will not suffer you to be tempted above that ye are able; but will with the temptation also make a way to escape, that ye may be able to bear it.

Wherefore let him that thinketh he standeth take heed lest he fall. There has no temptation taken you, but will with the temptation also make a way to escape, that ye may be able to bear it.

Luke 22:33, 42-43

> And he said unto him, Lord, I am ready to go with thee, both into prison, and to death. Saying, Father, if thou be willing, remove this cup from me: nevertheless not my will, but thine, be done. And there appeared an angel unto him from heaven, strengthening him.

We must rise and pray, lest we enter into temptation. When the Lord looked on Peter, Peter remembered the word of the Lord, that he would deny Him, and Peter went out and wept bitterly.

We must be honest with ourselves and with God, so that when our weakness or sin is revealed in our lives, we will face up to it and confess it to the Lord and ask Him to cleanse us.

We must be honest with ourselves and with God, so that when our weakness or sin is revealed in our lives, we will face up to it and confess it to the Lord and ask Him to cleanse us.

Proverbs 28:13

> He that covereth his sins shall not prosper: but whoso confesseth and forsaketh them shall have mercy.

Matthew 7:21

> Not every one that saith unto me, Lord, Lord, shall enter into the kingdom of heaven; but he that doeth the will of my Father which is in heaven.

Psalm 119:71-72

> It is good for me that I have been afflicted; that I might learn thy statutes. The law of thy mouth is better unto me than thousands of gold and silver.

My punishment was a good thing. It taught me to pay attention to you and your laws. Your laws are more valuable to me than silver and gold.

Strong acid alone will have no effect on gold. Fire will only purify it. It's the only metal improved by fire. Gold is so adaptable to shaping, it can be melted without harm, and it can be hammered to thin leaves, being extremely malleable. It may easily overlay large objects, thus imparting beauty and protection to the whole.

Strong acid alone will have no effect on gold. Fire will only purify it.

Revelation 21:15, 18, 21

> And he that talked with me had a golden reed to measure the city, and the gates thereof, and the wall thereof. And the building of the wall of it was of jasper: and the city was pure gold, like unto clear glass. And the twelve gates were twelve pearls: every several gate was of one pearl: and the street of the city

> was pure gold, as it were transparent glass.

In the Holy City, the streets were one of the most precious metals – gold – transparent as glass. The reed used to measure the city was a golden reed.

Job 28

> Surely there is a vein for the silver, and a place for gold where they fine it. Iron is taken out of the earth, and brass is molten out of the stone. He setteth an end to darkness, and searcheth out all perfection: the stones of darkness, and the shadow of death. The flood breaketh out from the inhabitant; even the waters forgotten of the foot: they are dried up, they are gone away from men. As for the earth, out of it cometh bread: and under it is turned up as it were fire. The stones of it are the place of sapphires: and it hath dust of gold.

In the Holy City, the streets were one of the most precious metals – gold – transparent as glass. The reed used to measure the city was a golden reed.

> There is a path which no fowl knoweth, and which the vulture's eye hath not seen: The lion's whelps have not trodden it, nor the fierce lion passed by it. He putteth forth his hand upon the rock; he overturneth the mountains by the roots. He cutteth out rivers

among the rocks; and his eye seeth every precious thing. He bindeth the floods from overflowing; and the thing that is hid bringeth he forth to light.

But where shall wisdom be found? and where is the place of understanding? Man knoweth not the price thereof; neither is it found in the land of the living. The depth saith, It is not in me: and the sea saith, It is not with me. It cannot be gotten for gold, neither shall silver be weighed for the price thereof. It cannot be valued with the gold of Ophir, with the precious onyx, or the sapphire. The gold and the crystal cannot equal it: and the exchange of it shall not be for jewels of fine gold. No mention shall be made of coral, or of pearls: for the price of wisdom is above rubies.

> Job points out that wisdom is so priceless that gold and silver and precious stones could not buy it.

The topaz of Ethiopia shall not equal it, neither shall it be valued with pure gold. Whence then cometh wisdom? and where is the place of understanding? Seeing it is hid from the eyes of all living, and kept close from the fowls of the air. Destruction and death say, We have heard the fame thereof with our ears.

God understandeth the way thereof, and he knoweth the place thereof. For he looketh to the ends of the earth, and seeth under the whole heaven; to make the

> weight for the winds; and he weigheth the waters by measure. When he made a decree for the rain, and a way for the lightning of the thunder: Then did he see it, and declare it; he prepared it, yea, and searched it out. And unto man he said, Behold, the fear of the Lord, that is wisdom; and to depart from evil is understanding.

The question of where wisdom should be found is in Job's words. He points out that wisdom is so priceless that gold and silver and precious stones could not buy it. It is a remarkable fact that gold is mentioned five times, while each of the other most precious items is mentioned but once.

The Value of the Blood

I Peter 1:18-19

> Forasmuch as ye know that ye were not redeemed with corruptible things, as silver and gold, from your vain conversation received by tradition from your fathers; But with the precious blood of Christ, as of a lamb without blemish and without spot:

You were not redeemed with corruptible things, as silver and gold . . . but with the Precious Blood of Christ.

When the Temple was dedicated on Mount Moriah, the actual count of animals slaughtered was amazing. Before the Ark of the Covenant was brought in, it is recorded that the sacrificing of sheep and oxen "could not be told nor numbered for multitude."

I Kings 8:5

> And king Solomon, and all the congregation of Israel, that were assembled unto him, were with him before the ark, sacrificing sheep and oxen, that could not be told nor numbered for multitude.

II Chronicles 5:6

> Also king Solomon, and all the congregation of Israel that were assembled unto him before the ark, sacrificed sheep and oxen, which could not be told nor numbered for multitude.

A peace offering was later made on behalf of the whole nation of Israel, and it is recorded that 22,000 oxen and 120,000 sheep were sacrificed. No "seconds" were good enough.

In I Kings 8 we are told that a peace offering was later made on behalf of the whole nation of Israel, and it is recorded that 22,000 oxen and 120,000 sheep were sacrificed. No "seconds" were good enough.

By this it seems God is trying to impress upon us that the value of the Blood cannot be measured in dollars, cents, or gallons. NO AMOUNT of blood of animals in the Old Testament could have atoned for our sins. On the Day of Atonement, the Brook Kidron was fed with the blood of animals that flowed continually for days, reminding the inhabitants of Jerusalem that when God caused His Son to die, He opened a fountain that would flow forever and ever.

Zechariah 13:1

> In that day there shall be a fountain opened to the house of David and to the inhabitants of Jerusalem for sin and for uncleanness.

This is described as a river, a continually flowing river into which we may plunge daily to wash away our sins and sicknesses and sorrows. This stream ever flows before Satan and all his hosts; and as we honor it, sing about it, talk about it, and plead it out loud, the *Blood of Jesus pleads mercy, forgiveness, pardon, healing protection, deliverance, and multiplied joy and peace.*

It is not enough to believe in an historic Blood of Calvary. It is necessary that we believe in the fountain NOW, and by faith avail ourselves of its power and life. Love is only a word until it is used. Ammunition in an arsenal is useless. It must be taken and used to bring terror to the enemy. The army of the Lord is powerless until it uses its weapons; these weapons are mighty to the bringing down of strongholds.

It is not enough to believe in an historic Blood of Calvary. It is necessary that we believe in the fountain NOW, and by faith avail ourselves of its power and life.

II Corinthians 10:4

> (For the weapons of our warfare are not carnal, but mighty through God to the pulling down of

> strong holds;)

They are the sword of the Spirit, which is the Word of God, and the Blood.

Revelation 12:11

> And they overcame him by the blood of the Lamb, and by the word of their testimony; and they loved not their lives unto the death.

We need the WORD and the BLOOD.

The sacrifices of King Solomon of the blood did not end the sacrifices. There were daily sacrifices, to remind the people of the present power of the blood. No "yesterday's leftovers" could be accepted. The same is true of the manna, which speaks of the WORD of God.

The sacrifices of King Solomon of the blood did not end the sacrifices. There were daily sacrifices, to remind the people of the present power of the blood. No "yesterday's leftovers" could be accepted.

Hebrews 9:22

> And almost all things are by the law purged with blood; and without shedding of blood is no remission.

Without the shedding of blood, there is no emission. It is

necessary for us to apply the Blood of Jesus daily.

Nothing could be obtained from God except by the blood sacrifice. It is impossible to compute the amount of blood that was shed in the 1,500 years of Israel's history under the old covenant.

The great Day of Atonement, held annually, with the scapegoat taken off into the wilderness, had great meaning as a type of Christ, who took the condemnation and curse of sin upon Himself, and carried it off into an uninhabited desert place, to be seen no more (Leviticus 22).

The Passover was repeated every year. If, for every fifteen people (an average for each household), a lamb was slain, then for two-and-a-half-million people at the time of the Exodus, over 160,000 lambs were slain on that historic night, when the bonds of Egypt gave way before the blood.

In the time of Solomon, the population had increased to five or six million, so the lambs slain then could have been around 400,000.

We now accept Jesus' sacrifice and offer His Blood by faith. Praise God for Jesus.

Nothing could be obtained from God except by the blood sacrifice. It is impossible to compute the amount of blood that was shed in the 1,500 years of Israel's history under the old covenant.

Jesus appeared unto Mary, first after His resurrection, and said to her, "Touch me not; for I am not yet ascended to My Father." (John 20:17) In the law of Israel, a High Priest could not be touched by the people just before he entered into the Holy Place with the blood of animals. It was only after he had offered blood and been accepted before the mercy seat, that the common people could touch him. In like manner, Jesus the High Priest could not be touched with human hands until He had ascended to His Father and offered His Blood at the throne of God. We assume this was done sometime in the next few days after appearing to Mary, for when He appeared to the other disciples a few days later, He said, "Behold my hands and my feet, that it is I myself: handle me, and see; for a spirit hath not flesh and bones, as ye see me have." (Luke 24:39)

In the law of Israel, a High Priest could not be touched by the people just before he entered into the Holy Place with the blood of animals. It was only after he had offered blood and been accepted before the mercy seat, that the common people could touch him.

Jesus' blood was accepted by God, for no other sacrifice would have been sufficient, except for His Own Precious Blood.

Now we can enter right into the Holy Place in Heaven, itself, anytime or place we want to. We can only come with the

Precious Blood of Jesus.

Hebrews 10:19-22

> Having therefore, brethren, boldness to enter into the holiest by the blood of Jesus, by a new and living way, which he hath consecrated for us, through the veil, that is to say, his flesh; and having an high priest over the house of God; let us draw near with a true heart in full assurance of faith, having our hearts sprinkled from an evil conscience, and our bodies washed with pure water.

The Scarlet Thread

Rahab the harlot was spared as well as her household with the scarlet thread, a type of the Blood of Christ.

The two Israelite spies found safety in the best place they could find – a brothel!

The city of Jericho was so wicked that God chose the Israelite army to wipe them off the face of the earth. Rahab began to confess to the two spies. She said, "For the Lord your God, he is God in heaven above, and in earth beneath." (Joshua 2:11)

She knew that Israel would win the battle, so she wanted to be saved as well as her whole household. She asked them to give her a TRUE TOKEN.

They told her that all of her family that were in the house would be saved. They remembered when the death angel passed over and saw the blood. They were saved. (Exodus

12:13)

Because of her faith, the Lamb of God slain from the foundation of the world became efficacious for this poor harlot and her sinning family. Jesus has no appeal to the worldly-wise and the self-righteous. He came to those who needed a physician.

Exodus 12:13

> And the blood shall be to you for a token upon the houses where ye are: and when I see the blood, I will pass over you, and the plague shall not be upon you to destroy you, when I smite the land of Egypt.

Because of her faith, the Lamb of God slain from the foundation of the world became efficacious for this poor harlot and her sinning family. Jesus has no appeal to the worldly-wise and the self-righteous. He came to those who needed a physician.

This speaks of the Blood of Jesus, already shed in the mind of the Father. (Revelation 13:8) Had they been able, they would have slain a lamb and sprinkled its blood on Rahab's home. They were being sought by the King of Jericho.

Joshua 2:18

> Behold, when we come into the land, thou shalt bind

> this line of scarlet thread in the window which thou didst let us down by: and thou shalt bring thy father, and thy mother, and thy brethren, and all thy father's household, home unto thee.

Hang the scarlet thread out the window honoring the Blood type. "Stay in your house! *If any go out, their blood will be on their own heads.*"

Joshua 2:21

> And she said, According unto your words, so be it. And she sent them away, and they departed: and she bound the scarlet line in the window.

According to thy words, be it so. Yes, there is a Blood line, and the Great Destroyer cannot get through it, but you must lay it in place.

Israelites, led by the singers, walked around the walls of Jericho for seven days. The wall of Rahab stood firm. The Israelites entered and set fire to everything except Rahab's house.

Israelites, led by the singers, walked around the walls of Jericho for seven days. The wall of Rahab stood firm. The Israelites entered and set fire to everything except Rahab's house. They then joined the Israelites and *by faith became a part.* Like we do today – by faith.

Even many years before this, when the High Priest was ordained to the priesthood, part of his ordination included putting blood upon his right ear, the thumb of his right hand, and his big toe on his right foot. The blood kept Satan away from his thoughts, his work, and where he traveled.

When the Blood is applied by faith today, it is just as powerful for us as it was to Moses or Joshua.

We are not to let down our faith in the Precious Blood of Jesus. There is more power in the Blood than anyone has ever imagined.

We must realize that Satan is the author of all damage to the body. The Blood of Jesus is the finest covering and disinfectant in the world. It is perfect.

A Better Testament

Our Lord is raised up by the very Word of the Lord God in Heaven.

Hebrews 7:22

> By so much was Jesus made a surety of a better testament.

Hebrews 7:24

> But this man, because he continueth ever, hath an unchangeable priesthood.

Hebrews 7:27

> Who needeth not daily, as those high priests, to offer up sacrifice, first for his own sins, and then for the people's: for this he did once, when he offered up himself.

Hebrews 7:28

For the law maketh men high priests which have infirmity; but the word of the oath, which was since the law, maketh the Son, who is consecrated (PERFECT) for evermore.

Hebrews 8:6

But now hath he obtained a more excellent ministry, by how much also he is the mediator of a better covenant, which was established upon better promises.

Hebrews 8:8

For finding fault with them, he saith, Behold, the days come, saith the Lord, when I will make a new covenant with the house of Israel and with the house of Judah:

Hebrews 9:7

But into the second went the high priest alone once every year, not without blood, which he offered for himself, and for the errors of the people:

Hebrews 9:24

For Christ is not entered into the holy places made with hands, which are the figures of the true; but into heaven itself, now to appear in the presence of God for us:

In the Shelter of His Arms

Sadness does not separate us from Jesus.

Even when we are filled with sorrow, we can remain in the flow of the Holy Ghost.

Our grief does not mean we are outside the will of God.

The same Spirit that moved Jesus will move us if we know the full flow of the Spirit.

He sends us forth as lambs (our evident suffering).

John 15

> I am the true vine, and my Father is the husbandman. Every branch in me that beareth not fruit he taketh away: and every branch that beareth fruit, he purgeth it, that it may bring forth more fruit. Now ye are clean through the word which I have spoken unto you.
>
> Abide in me, and I in you. As the branch cannot bear

fruit of itself, except it abide in the vine; no more can ye, except ye abide in me. I am the vine, ye are the branches: He that abideth in me, and I in him, the same bringeth forth much fruit: for without me ye can do nothing. If a man abide not in me, he is cast forth as a branch, and is withered; and men gather them, and cast them into the fire, and they are burned. If ye abide in me, and my words abide in you, ye shall ask what ye will, and it shall be done unto you.

The same Spirit that moved Jesus will move us if we know the full flow of the Spirit.

Herein is my Father glorified, that ye bear much fruit; so shall ye be my disciples. As the Father hath loved me, so have I loved you: continue ye in my love. If ye keep my commandments, ye shall abide in my love; even as I have kept my Father's commandments, and abide in his love. These things have I spoken unto you, that my joy might remain in you, and that your joy might be full.

This is my commandment, that ye love one another, as I have loved you. Greater love hath no man than this, that a man lay down his life for his friends. Ye are my friends, if ye do whatsoever I command you. Henceforth I call you not servants; for the servant knoweth not what his lord doeth: but I have called you friends; for all things that I have heard of my Father I have made known unto you. Ye have not chosen me, but I have chosen you, and ordained you, that ye should go and bring forth fruit, and that your fruit should remain: that whatsoever ye shall ask of the Father in my name, he may give it you.

These things I command you, that ye love one another. If the world hate you, ye know that it hated me before it hated you. If ye were of the world, the world would love his own: but because ye are not of the world, but I have chosen you out of the world, therefore the world hateth you. Remember the word that I said unto you, the servant is not greater than his lord. If they have persecuted me, they will also persecute you; if they have kept my saying, they will keep yours also. But all these things will they do unto you for my name's sake, because they know not him that sent me.

> That My joy may be in you, that your joy may be full. It's linked to bearing fruit (being fruitful). The key to the nature of joy is being fruitful.

If I had not come and spoken unto them, they had not had sin: but now they have no cloak for their sin. He that hateth me hateth my Father also. If I had not done among them the works which none other man

> did, they had not had sin: but now have they both seen and hated both me and my Father.
>
> But this cometh to pass, that the word might be fulfilled that is written in their law, they hated me without a cause. But when the Comforter is come, whom I will send unto you from the Father, even the Spirit of truth, which proceedeth from the Father, he shall testify of me: And ye also shall bear witness, because ye have been with me from the beginning.

That My joy may be in you, that your joy may be full. It's linked to bearing fruit (being fruitful). The key to the nature of joy is being fruitful. As Jesus hung on the cross with the sorrows of humanity on Him, He was conscious of the joy of the Father within Him.

As Jesus hung on the cross with the sorrows of humanity on Him, He was conscious of the joy of the Father within Him.

Isaiah 53

> Who hath believed our report? and to whom is the arm of the Lord revealed? For he shall grow up before him as a tender plant, and as a root out of a dry ground: he hath no form nor comeliness; and when we shall see him, there is no beauty that we should desire him. He is despised and rejected of men; a man of sorrows, and acquainted with grief: and we hid as

it were our faces from him; he was despised, and we esteemed him not. Surely he hath borne our griefs, and carried our sorrows: yet we did esteem him stricken, smitten of God, and afflicted. But he was wounded for our transgressions, he was bruised for our iniquities: the chastisement of our peace was upon him; and with his stripes we are healed.

All we like sheep have gone astray; we have turned every one to his own way; and the Lord hath laid on him the iniquity of us all. He was oppressed, and he was afflicted, yet he opened not his mouth: he is brought as a lamb to the slaughter, and as a sheep before her shearers is dumb, so he openeth not his mouth. He was taken from prison and from judgment: and who shall declare his generation? for he was cut off out of the land of the living: for the transgression of my people was he stricken. And he made his grave with the wicked, and with the rich in his death; because he had done no violence, neither was any deceit in his mouth. Yet it pleased the Lord to bruise him; he hath put him to grief: when thou shalt make his soul an offering for sin, he shall see his seed, he shall prolong his days, and the pleasure of the Lord shall prosper in his hand.

> He shall see His seed (the travail of his soul). His joy is ours (We are his joy).

> He shall see of the travail of his soul, and shall be satisfied: by his knowledge shall my righteous servant justify many; for he shall bear their iniquities. Therefore will I divide him a portion with the great, and he shall divide the spoil with the strong; because he hath poured out his soul unto death: and he was numbered with the transgressors; and he bare the sin of many, and made intercession for the transgressors.

It pleased the Lord to bruise Him. He shall see His seed (the travail of his soul). His joy is ours (We are his joy). Jesus knew the disciples were going to go through deep travails. Sin brought upon woman the travails of childbearing. Yet, the birth of the child evaporates the memory of what has come before.

Sin brings great agony, but your sorrow will be turned into joy, which no man can take away from you.

This body is the source of corruption – we long to be delivered from this struggle. We groan within ourselves to be free.

This body is the source of corruption – we long to be delivered from this struggle. We groan within ourselves to be free.

II Thessalonians 2:1-7

> Now we beseech you, brethren, by the coming of our Lord Jesus Christ, and by our gathering together unto

> him, that ye be not soon shaken in mind, or be troubled, neither by spirit, nor by word, nor by letter as from us, as that the day of Christ is at hand. Let no man deceive you by any means: for that day shall not come, except there come a falling away first, and that man of sin be revealed, the son of perdition;
>
> Who opposeth and exalteth himself above all that is called God, or that is worshipped; so that he as God sitteth in the temple of God, shewing himself that he is God. Remember ye not, that, when I was yet with you, I told you these things? And now ye know what withholdeth that he might be revealed in his time. For the mystery of iniquity doth already work: only he who now letteth will let, until he be taken out of the way.

Paul so identified himself with the people in their need, it caused him sorrow and deep anguish until he saw them come into the fullness of the Spirit.

Parenthood – the Life of Christ in people. We have been called to bring forth fruit.

II Thessalonians 2:9-12

> Even him, whose coming is after the working of Satan with all power and signs and lying wonders, and with all deceivableness of unrighteousness in them

> that perish; because they received not the love of the truth, that they might be saved. And for this cause God shall send them strong delusion, that they should believe a lie: That they all might be damned who believed not the truth, but had pleasure in unrighteousness.

We see how he brought them to birth in Christ. Paul so identified himself with the people in their need, it caused him sorrow and deep anguish until he saw them come into the fullness of the Spirit. Until Christ be conceived in them and be brought to birth, he knew pain, then when it was brought to birth, his sorrow turned into joy.

Joy has very little to do with big smiles and laughter.

Children are our joy. Once you start loving people, you open yourself up to hurts. We become vulnerable by loving people. Our suffering can become the joy of the Lord.

Jesus on the Tree

It is doubtful if the Roman soldiers left Jesus even a loin cloth. He became as the first Adam in the garden. We might say He covered himself with His Own Blood. In turn, we may cover our nakedness with His Precious Blood, a perfect atonement or covering, indeed. We must come to Him as naked and destitute of all covering in His presence. Then, He will give us His own blessed robe of righteousness after we have accepted the cleansing of His Precious Blood.

First the thorns were pierced into His head, causing the blood to run down His face and into His hair and beard.

The spikes were driven into His palms – causing the blood to run down His arms and sides – and onto the ground.

The spear pierced His side.

The nails were driven into His feet causing even more of that Precious Blood to flow for all mankind to be cleansed from sin.

Psalms 22 describes the crucifixion. Our Lord's bones were out of joint, as He hung upon the tree.

Isaiah 53:2

> For he shall grow up before him as a tender plant, and as a root out of a dry ground: he hath no form nor comeliness; and when we shall see him, there is no beauty that we should desire him.

Our Lord had no beauty that we should desire Him. God gave His very BEST, His Son, His perfect sacrifice, and even in death, there was no blemish in Him. Those that looked upon Him saw only blood.

His back was lacerated by the thirty-nine stripes and was covered with His Own Blood, and the very earth was soaked. Every type of atonement was fulfilled in Christ; it was blood, blood, blood.

His back was lacerated by the thirty-nine stripes and was covered with His Own Blood, and the very earth was soaked. Every type of atonement was fulfilled in Christ; it was blood, blood, blood.

A complete atonement is provided in the Blood of Jesus Christ.

The word atonement is a beautiful word which means a covering. Where sin did abound, grace did much more abound, for with grace came the Blood of Jesus, which covers all our sins. If we can clearly understand the meaning of the word "atonement," we have discovered tremendous truth. God has provided a substance by which we can cover things we no longer want; God guarantees not even to see our sins after we reckon by faith that the Blood of Jesus has covered them. When God sees Blood, He does not see sin.

After it was accomplished, the Father then looked, not on our sins, but on His Son's Blood. That was enough. His Son had offered His life in His Blood for all mankind. The Father had respect unto the offering, and our redemption was made complete.

If we honor the Blood of Jesus Christ, the Father will smile upon us with forgiveness and cleansing.

This must be a very real and honest embracing of the Blood of Jesus – never methodically or only with the mind.

When God sees the Blood of His Son that we are offering for a covering, pardon or plea, He can only see the covering – the Blood. "It is the Blood that maketh an atonement for the soul."

Leviticus 17:11

> For the life of the flesh is in the blood: and I have given it to you upon the altar to make an atonement for your souls: for it is the blood that maketh an atonement for the soul.

Spirit, Water, and Blood

In the beginning, God commanded that living creatures be slain so that Adam and Eve could have a covering – which came by blood.

I John 5:8

> And there are three that bear witness in earth, the Spirit, and the water, and the blood: and these three agree in one.

Water is the Word of God. It is that which washes us continually.

Ephesians 5:26

> That he might sanctify and cleanse it with the washing of water by the word,

But the word without the BLOOD is ineffectual, for the life of Jesus, the WORD of God, is in the BLOOD.

This is why we partake of the bread and wine in communion. It speaks of Jesus, the crucified WORD of God, and the BLOOD, which He willingly shed.

The Holy Spirit is in complete agreement with the water and the Blood. For this reason, when we honor the Blood, the Holy Spirit immediately manifests His life on our behalf. *They are triunely one.*

> Jesus was crucified at the time of the feast of the Passover, the feast the Jews kept to remember the time when God said, "When I see the Blood, I will pass over you."

In the Old Testament times, on the Day of Atonement, the blood was sprinkled on the Book. The Book is a lifeless Book to the readers unless the Blood is first applied. Both the Book (Word of God) and the people were sprinkled with the blood. This, too, was fulfilled on Calvary. Jesus who is the Living Word of God, was sprinkled with His Own Blood.

Some think it is enough to have or use the name of Jesus, but not so. We need the name of Jesus and the Blood of Jesus, for the life is in the Blood. There is power in the name of Jesus, only because He shed His Own Blood and offered it to His Father, who thereupon gave His power and His authority to His Son.

Matthew 28:18

And Jesus came and spoke unto them, saying, All

> power is given unto me in heaven and in earth.

Luke 10:19

> Behold, I give unto you power to tread on serpents and scorpions, and over all the power of the enemy: and nothing shall by any means hurt you.

That same power is given to all believers, but it only becomes operative as we honor the Blood.

Hebrews 9:22

> And almost all things are by the law purged with blood; and without shedding of blood is no remission.

In the Old Testament, there always had to be blood shed from perfect animals for cleansing of sin – for atonements, for coverings. Jesus was crucified at the time of the feast of the Passover, the feast the Jews kept to remember the time when God said, "When I see the blood, I will pass over you."

Exodus 12:23

> For the Lord will pass through to smite the Egyptians; and when he seeth the blood upon the lintel, and on the two side posts, the Lord will pass over the door, and will not suffer the destroyer to come in unto your houses to smite you.

The Passover

Abram offered a ram.

Genesis 22:13

> And Abraham lifted up his eyes, and looked, and behold behind him a ram caught in a thicket by his horns: and Abraham went and took the ram, and offered him up for a burnt offering in the stead of his son.

Noah built an altar after the flood and offered some of every clean beast and fowl. These animals were costly; nothing cheap was good enough.

Genesis 8:20

> And Noah builded an altar unto the Lord; and took of every clean beast, and of every clean fowl, and offered burnt offerings on the altar.

God can only receive us and our thanksgiving on the grounds of the Blood of His Son. There is no other way into God's presence.

Because God provided a ram for sacrifice instead of the life of Isaac, the future was changed. Had Isaac not been spared, there would not be an Israel today. Isaac was Abraham's only son, so Isaac was a miraculously delivered child, saved by blood. Every Israelite knew this story and understood the blood.

Also, they knew this from Egyptian bondage – it took the blood to turn the battle in favor of God's people.

God can only receive us and our thanksgiving on the grounds of the Blood of His Son. There is no other way into God's presence.

Exodus 12:3-14

> Speak ye unto all the congregation of Israel, saying, In the tenth day of this month they shall take to them every man a lamb, according to the house of their fathers, a lamb for an house: and if the household be too little for the lamb, let him and his neighbour next unto his house take it according to the number of the souls; every man according to his eating shall make your count for the lamb. Your lamb shall be without blemish, a male of the first year: ye shall take it out from the sheep, or from the goats: and ye shall keep it up until the fourteenth day of the same month: and the whole

assembly of the congregation of Israel shall kill it in the evening.

And they shall take of the blood, and strike it on the two side posts and on the upper door post of the houses, wherein they shall eat it. And they shall eat the flesh in that night, roast with fire, and unleavened bread; and with bitter herbs they shall eat it. Eat not of it raw, nor sodden at all with water, but roast with fire; his head with his legs, and with the purtenance thereof. And ye shall let nothing of it remain until the morning; and that which remaineth of it until the morning ye shall burn with fire.

> "And they shall take of the blood, and strike it on the two side posts and on the upper door post of the houses, wherein they shall eat it. And they shall eat the flesh in that night, roast with fire, and unleavened bread; and with bitter herbs they shall eat it."

And thus shall ye eat it; with your loins girded, your shoes on your feet, and your staff in your hand; and ye shall eat it in haste: it is the Lord's passover. For I will pass through the land of Egypt this night, and will smite all the first-born in the land of Egypt, both man and beast; and against all the gods of Egypt I will execute judgment: I am the Lord. And the blood

> shall be to you for a token upon the houses where ye are: and when I see the blood, I will pass over you, and the plague shall not be upon you to destroy you, when I smite the land of Egypt.
>
> And this day shall be unto you for a memorial; and ye shall keep it a feast to the Lord throughout your generations; ye shall keep it a feast by an ordinance for ever.

A lamb for each house, about 15 people. God wants to save whole families. God promises, "I WILL PASS OVER YOU."

> "For the Lord will pass through to smite the Egyptians; and when he seeth the blood upon the lintel, and on the two side posts, the Lord will pass over the door, and will not suffer the destroyer to come in unto your houses to smite you."

Exodus 12:22-27

> And ye shall take a bunch of hyssop, and dip it in the blood that is in the bason, and strike the lintel and the two side posts with the blood that is in the bason; and none of you shall go out at the door of his house until the morning. For the Lord will pass through to smite the Egyptians; and when he seeth the blood upon the lintel, and on the two side posts, the Lord will pass over the door, and will not suffer the destroyer to come in unto your houses to smite

> you. And ye shall observe this thing for an ordinance to thee and to thy sons for ever.
>
> And it shall come to pass, when ye be come to the land which the Lord will give you, according as he hath promised, that ye shall keep this service. And it shall come to pass, when your children shall say unto you, What mean ye by this service? That ye shall say, It is the sacrifice of the Lord's passover, who passed over the houses of the children of Israel in Egypt, when he smote the Egyptians, and delivered our houses. And the people bowed the head and worshipped.

He will not suffer the destroyer to come in unto your houses to smite you.

God's orders are to obeyed perfectly.

Satan is both ruler of this world and the prince of the upper atmosphere that surrounds this earth. It is only the mercy of God that keeps us from the incredible power of the wicked destroying angel, Satan.

The destroyer is none other than Satan.

Job was attacked by this destroyer only by God's permission. Even so, God worked it out for Job's good in the end.

Ephesians 2:2

Wherein in time past ye walked according to the

> course of this world, according to the prince of the power of the air, the spirit that now worketh in the children of disobedience:

Satan is both ruler of this world and the prince of the upper atmosphere that surrounds this earth. It is only the mercy of God that keeps us from the incredible power of the wicked destroying angel, Satan. It is only faith in the Blood of Jesus that comes between us, the devil and his demon spirits.

Count It All Joy

James 1:2-4

> My brethren, count it all joy when ye fall into divers temptations; Knowing this, that the trying of your faith worketh patience. But let patience have her perfect work, that ye may be perfect and entire, wanting nothing.

James 1:12

> Blessed is the man that endureth temptation: for when he is tried, he shall receive the crown of life, which the Lord hath promised to them that love him.

Just because you have grief or sorrow, you are not out of the flow of the Spirit.

Hebrews 12:2-3

> Looking unto Jesus the author and finisher of our

> faith; who for the joy that was set before him endured the cross, despising the shame, and is set down at the right hand of the throne of God. For consider him that endured such contradiction of sinners against himself, lest ye be wearied and faint in your minds.

Jesus endured the cross for the joy that was set before Him.

Hebrews 12:11

> Now no chastening for the present seemeth to be joyous, but grievous: nevertheless afterward it yieldeth the peaceable fruit of righteousness unto them which are exercised thereby.

Jesus endured the cross for the joy that was set before Him.

Acts 20:22-24

> And now, behold, I go bound in the spirit unto Jerusalem, not knowing the things that shall befall me there: Save that the Holy Ghost witnesseth in every city, saying that bonds and afflictions abide me. But none of these things move me, neither count I my life dear unto myself, so that I might finish my course with joy, and the ministry, which I have received of the Lord Jesus, to testify the gospel of the grace of God.

Paul knew what awaited him in Jerusalem, but with joy, he was determined to finish his course.

II Timothy 4:6-8

> For I am now ready to be offered, and the time of my departure is at hand. I have fought a good fight, I have finished my course, I have kept the faith: Henceforth there is laid up for me a crown of righteousness, which the Lord, the righteous judge, shall give me at that day: and not to me only, but unto all them also that love his appearing.

Paul fought a good fight. He finished his course. He kept the faith, and a crown of righteousness was laid up for him.

Jesus was in the presence of the Hebrew children in their trial. He will always be with us to take us through. We sometimes cry, "Take us out!" but He takes us through – and causes us to be made more like Him.

Jesus was in the presence of the Hebrew children in their trial. He will always be with us to take us through. We sometimes cry, "Take us out!" but He takes us through – and causes us to be made more like Him.

Jude 24-25

> Now unto him that is able to keep you from falling, and to present you faultless before the presence of his glory with exceeding joy, to the only wise God our Saviour, be glory and majesty, dominion and power, both now and ever. Amen.

Jesus will present us to God with exceeding joy. On the cross, we were the pain which Jesus suffered. In glory, we will be the joy He will have. Our worship is joy to Jesus.

I Peter 4:12-13

> Beloved, think it not strange concerning the fiery trial which is to try you, as though some strange thing happened unto you: But rejoice, inasmuch as ye are partakers of Christ's sufferings; that, when his glory shall be revealed, ye may be glad also with exceeding joy.

Psalm 30:5

> For his anger endureth but a moment; in his favour is life: weeping may endure for a night, but joy cometh in the morning.

Jesus will present us to God with exceeding joy. On the cross, we were the pain which Jesus suffered. In glory, we will be the joy He will have.

Psalm 16:11

> Thou wilt shew me the path of life: in thy presence is fulness of joy; at thy right hand there are pleasures for evermore.

Nehemiah 8:10

> Then he said unto them, Go your way, eat the fat, and drink the sweet, and send portions unto them for

> whom nothing is prepared: for this day is holy unto our Lord: neither be ye sorry; for the joy of the Lord is your strength.

Psalm 126:5-6

> They that sow in tears shall reap in joy. He that goeth forth and weepeth, bearing precious seed, shall doubtless come again with rejoicing, bringing his sheaves with him.

Isaiah 12:2

> Behold, God is my salvation; I will trust, and not be afraid: for the Lord Jehovah is my strength and my song; he also is become my salvation.

If we complain and are critical in trials, they will seem worse and be drawn out longer. We should sing praises and bless the Lord in the height of our problems. Even if it doesn't change our circumstances, it will change our attitude and emotions. We will feel better, and most of the time what is troubling us will change.

We should endure for the joy that is set before us: Heaven. (Mark 8:31-33)

Life Is in the Blood

Genesis 2:7

> And the Lord God formed man of the dust of the ground, and breathed into his nostrils the breath of life; and man became a living soul.

God created man and breathed into him the breath of life.

Psalms 139:14

> I will praise thee; for I am fearfully and wonderfully made: marvellous are thy works; and that my soul knoweth right well.

Man is fearfully and wonderfully made.

When God made man, He formed a body from the dust of the ground, from the substances and chemicals of this planet. Then He breathed into this body the breath of life. He breathed into this chemical composition some of His own spiritual life, and that life was held in the chemical substance we call blood.

Blood is not life, but it carries life.

When a person dies, they remain warm for a brief time. Yet, the person is dead because the mysterious life has departed from the blood. The life of man is carried in his bloodstream. Life itself is spiritual, but it must have a physical carrier, and that carrier is the blood.

The most amazing thing about blood is its capacity to carry the life of God. The contact between the Devine and the human rests in the bloodstream. Blood can even be frozen and thawed, and the life in it not be affected.

The life of man is carried in his bloodstream. Life itself is spiritual, but it must have a physical carrier, and that carrier is the blood.

The Blood that flowed in His veins was perfect, for it was not contaminated by Adam's sin, which brought sin and sickness into human blood.

If Adam had not sinned, he would not have died.

Jesus Christ had no sin in His body, but He allowed Himself to die for the sins of a sinful humanity. He gave the perfect life that was in His perfect Blood to redeem poor mankind, who carried death in their bodies – pure Blood for imperfect, contaminated blood – life for life, for the life is in the blood.

This is why Jesus is described as the last Adam. God sent Him to earth in the *likeness* of sinful Adam, but with pure, uncontaminated Blood in His veins. God sent Him so that He might shed that pure Blood of His for the life of humanity.

I Peter 1:19

> But with the precious blood of Christ, as of a lamb without blemish and without spot:

Peter describes it as *Precious Blood.* It is God's price for the redemption of the whole human race. Jesus' Blood could not have been typed or categorized like ours.

Joel 3:21

> For I will cleanse their blood that I have not cleansed: for the Lord dwelleth in Zion.

When we receive the Lord, the Bible declares that the heart is cleansed by the Blood of Jesus. When sin is gone, the heart can be cleansed.

When we receive the Lord, the Bible declares that the heart is cleansed by the Blood of Jesus. When sin is gone, the heart can be cleansed.

The greatest disinfectant in the world is the Blood of Jesus Christ. It carries the eternal life of God in it.

Satan's nickname is Beelzebub, meaning "Lord of the Flies," or "Prince of the Flies." Dead blood will quickly attract flies, which will breed corruption in the coagulating blood; but the Blood of Jesus has exactly the opposite effect: it *repulses* Beelzebub and all his demons. When you put the blood of Jesus on something by faith, Satan will flee, because the Blood of Jesus is alive. The life is in the Blood.

The devil hates the mention of Jesus and/or the Blood of Jesus.

Blood does not control the color of the skin or the culture of the person.

It is possible for a person to bleed to death. As soon as the blood is gone, the life is gone.

It is possible for a person to bleed to death. As soon as the blood is gone, the life is gone.

This discussion quite naturally leads to some consideration of the unique nature of Jesus' Blood.

The female ovum itself has no blood; neither has the male spermatozoon; but it is when these come together in the fallopian tube that conception takes place, and a new life begins. The blood cells in this new creation are from both the father and mother, and the blood type is determined at the moment of conception and is thereafter protected by the placenta from any flow of the mother's blood into the fetus.

The Bible is explicit that the Holy Spirit was the Devine Agent who caused Jesus' conception in the *womb of Mary.*

It is inconceivable that Mary could have supplied any of her Adamic blood for the spotless Lamb of God.

This, therefore, was not a normal conception, but a supernatural act of God in planting the life of His already existent Son right in the womb of Mary, with no normal conception of a male spermatozoon with the female ovum of Mary. As the blood type of the Son of God was a separate and precious type, it is inconceivable that Mary could have supplied any of her Adamic blood for the spotless Lamb of God. All the child's blood came from His Father in Heaven by a supernatural creative act of God. Jesus' Blood was without the Adamic stain of sin.

Hebrews 10:1-14

> For the law having a shadow of good things to come, and not the very image of the things, can never with those sacrifices which they offered year by year continually make the comers thereunto perfect. For then would they not have ceased to be offered? because that the worshippers once purged should have had no more conscience of sins. But in those sacrifices there is a remembrance again made of sins every year. For it is not possible that the blood of bulls and of goats should take away sins. Wherefore when he cometh into the world, he saith, Sacrifice and offering thou wouldest not, but a body hast thou prepared me: In

burnt offerings and sacrifices for sin thou hast had no pleasure.

Then said I, Lo, I come (in the volume of the book it is written of me,) to do thy will, O God. Above when he said, Sacrifice and offering and burnt offerings and offering for sin thou wouldest not, neither hadst pleasure therein; which are offered by the law; then said he, Lo, I come to do thy will, O God. He taketh away the first, that he may establish the second. By the which will we are sanctified through the offering of the body of Jesus Christ once for all.

> The LIFE that was in Jesus Christ came alone from the FATHER by the Holy Ghost. No wonder He said, "I AM THE LIFE."

And every priest standeth daily ministering and offering oftentimes the same sacrifices, which can never take away sins: But this man, after he had offered one sacrifice for sins for ever, sat down on the right hand of God; From henceforth expecting till his enemies be made his footstool. For by one offering he hath perfected for ever them that are sanctified.

God prepared a body for Jesus right in the womb of Mary.

John 1:14

And the Word was made flesh, and dwelt among us,

(and we beheld his glory, the glory as of the only begotten of the Father,) full of grace and truth.

Jesus was the only begotten of His Father. The LIFE that was in Jesus Christ came alone from the FATHER by the Holy Ghost. No wonder He said, "I AM THE LIFE."

Luke 1:47

And my spirit hath rejoiced in God my Saviour.

Mary declared her son was "GOD MY SAVIOR." At the very time the Jews were celebrating the first exodus, Jesus was making atonement for the second exodus. To all who will believe in this sacrifice and the power of His Precious Blood, there is an exodus from sin and the penalty of sin, which includes sickness and bondage.

At the very time the Jews were celebrating the first exodus, Jesus was making atonement for the second exodus.

Jesus sprinkled His Own Blood and fulfilled the following archetypes:

- On the cross (Exodus 24:6-8)
- Round about the cross (Exodus 29:12-16)
- High Priest's garments (Exodus 29:20-21)
- Sprinkled seven times for perfection (Leviticus 4:6-7)
- Bottom of the cross (Leviticus 4:6-7)
- Side of the cross (Leviticus 5:9)

- Round about the cross and on the earth beneath the cross (Leviticus 7:2)
- Sprinkled before the tabernacle seven times (Numbers 19:4)

The cross and hill of Calvary were within sight of the Temple in Jerusalem, for Calvary was outside of the city.

All these Old Testament types were fulfilled in the crucifixion of Jesus, who made Himself our Passover, our Vicar, our Savior, and our Blood sacrifice. His Blood alone covers our sins.

It is no wonder Jesus cried out to His Father when He took upon Himself all the sins of the whole world. "My God, My God, why hast thou forsaken me?" (Psalms 22:1 and Matthew 27:46)

It is no wonder Jesus cried out to His Father when He took upon Himself all the sins of the whole world. "My God, My God, why hast thou forsaken me?"

Why had the Father forsaken Him?

Habakkuk 1:13

> Thou art of purer eyes than to behold evil, and canst not look on iniquity: wherefore lookest thou upon them that deal treacherously, and holdest thy tongue when the wicked devoureth the man that is more righteous than he?

God cannot look upon evil or sin. When Jesus was bearing the sins of the world in His body upon the cross, His Father could not look at His Son. Jesus had become sin for us. When Jesus' Blood covered His body with His Blood, then the Father could look upon Him.

He had been obedient unto death, even the death of the cross, and now our sins were atoned for or covered, under His Precious Blood. His life for our life – that is what the Father demanded.

Do not underestimate the power of the Blood of Jesus.

Leviticus 17:11

> For the life of the flesh is in the blood: and I have given it to you upon the altar to make an atonement for your souls: for it is the blood that maketh an atonement for the soul.

He had been obedient unto death, even the death of the cross, and now our sins were atoned for or covered, under His Precious Blood. His life for our life – that is what the Father demanded.

Hebrews 9:22

> And almost all things are by the law purged with blood; and without shedding of blood is no remission.

The Spirit of Rejection

Mark 11:12, 21-22, 25

And on the morrow, when they were come from Bethany, he was hungry: And Peter calling to remembrance saith unto him, Master, behold, the fig tree which thou cursedst is withered away. And Jesus answering saith unto them, Have faith in God. And when ye stand praying, forgive, if ye have ought against any: that your Father also which is in heaven may forgive you your trespasses.

Matthew 6:14

For if ye forgive men their trespasses, your heavenly Father will also forgive you:

Psalm 147:3

He healeth the broken in heart, and bindeth up their wounds.

John 10:10

> The thief cometh not, but for to steal, and to kill, and to destroy: I am come that they might have life, and that they might have it more abundantly.

We have to get at the root cause. If you pray for headaches, pray for the root cause.

Somewhere in the past, we were rejected by someone, and probably we forgot it, but the hurt is still there.

Somewhere in the past, we were rejected by someone, and probably we forgot it, but the hurt is still there.

Maybe someone made fun of you and hurt you. In drawing back, we add another scar to the wound.

People, parents, sisters and brothers, teachers, and the church. The spirit of rejection opens the door for other spirits.

The enemy will cause our minds to pick them up (most of the time they are lies) but then the unconscious mind receives it.

Some sicknesses are caused from unforgiveness.

God always forgives us when we ask. We need to forgive ourselves.

Rejection can cause these things:

- Fears of all kinds
- Lust of the flesh and other things
- Bitterness
- Masturbation
- Frustration
- Divorce
- Children that have been sexually abused
- Spirit of division
- Hatred
- Emotional deadness
- Inferiority

Our Watchtower

Isaiah 61:1, 3

> The Spirit of the Lord God is upon me; because the Lord hath anointed me to preach good tidings unto the meek; he hath sent me to bind up the broken-hearted, to proclaim liberty to the captives, and the opening of the prison to them that are bound;

John 15:1-8

> I am the true vine, and my Father is the husbandman. Every branch in me that beareth not fruit he taketh away: and every branch that beareth fruit, he purgeth it, that it may bring forth more fruit. Now ye are clean through the word which I have spoken unto you. Abide in me, and I in you. As the branch cannot bear fruit of itself, except it abide in the vine; no more can ye, except ye abide in me.

> I am the vine, ye are the branches: He that abideth in me, and I in him, the same bringeth forth much fruit: for without me ye can do nothing. If a man abide not in me, he is cast forth as a branch, and is withered; and men gather them, and cast them into the fire, and they are burned. If ye abide in me, and my words abide in you, ye shall ask what ye will, and it shall be done unto you. Herein is my Father glorified, that ye bear much fruit; so shall ye be my disciples.

Jesus is the true vine. He was planted in the earth. A vine planted will spread. Jesus is being spread all over the earth.

Jesus is the true vine. He was planted in the earth. A vine planted will spread. Jesus is being spread all over the earth.

The vine is attached to the root. The believer is the branches.

Romans 11:18

> Boast not against the branches. But if thou boast, thou bearest not the root, but the root thee.

For the branch to grow, there must be sap from the roots to give nourishment. We grow in grace. The more we grow, the more we can see accomplishments in our lives.

The vineyard had to be protected – a costly investment. God’s costly investment was His Son.

The watchtower is our intercessor.

II Chronicles 16:9

> For the eyes of the Lord run to and fro throughout the whole earth, to shew himself strong in the behalf of them whose heart is perfect toward him. Herein thou hast done foolishly: therefore from henceforth thou shalt have wars.

If your heart is blameless, you can know He is watching over you. The believer who has turned his back on Jesus is the one who has been a branch, but has stopped believing or producing fruit.

If your heart is blameless, you can know He is watching over you. The believer who has turned his back on Jesus is the one who has been a branch, but has stopped believing or producing fruit.

Hebrews 6:4-8

> For it is impossible for those who were once enlightened, and have tasted of the heavenly gift, and were made partakers of the Holy Ghost, And have tasted the good word of God, and the powers of the world to come, If they shall fall away, to renew them again unto repentance; seeing they crucify to themselves the Son of God afresh, and put him to an open shame. For the earth which drinketh in the rain that cometh oft upon it, and bringeth forth herbs meet for them by whom it is dressed, receiveth blessing

> from God: But that which beareth thorns and briers is rejected, and is nigh unto cursing; whose end is to be burned.

People who profess to believe in Christ but don't are dead branches.

Jeremiah 17:10

> I the Lord search the heart, I try the reins, even to give every man according to his ways, and according to the fruit of his doings.

In Him I live, I move, and have my being. The branch clings to the vine. We should cling to him, loving the Lord with all our might and strength and heart and soul.

Acts 17:28

> For in him we live, and move, and have our being; as certain also of your own poets have said, For we are also his offspring.

In Him I live, I move, and have my being. The branch clings to the vine. We should cling to him, loving the Lord with all our might and strength and heart and soul.

Deuteronomy 6:5-6

> And thou shalt love the Lord thy God with all thine heart, and with all thy soul, and with all thy might. And these words, which I command thee this day, shall be in thine heart:

John 5:19

> Then answered Jesus and said unto them, Verily, verily, I say unto you, The Son can do nothing of himself, but what he seeth the Father do: for what things soever he doeth, these also doeth the Son likewise.

The Father's support never fails on His part. It is up to us to keep it flowing from the vine to the branches. He is the support in the root.

Philippians 4:13

> I can do all things through Christ which strengtheneth me.

He is the one who infuses the inner strength into us.

The Father's support never fails on His part. It is up to us to keep it flowing from the vine to the branches. He is the support in the root.

Matthew 22:8

> Then saith he to his servants, The wedding is ready, but they which were bidden were not worthy.

We do not know the intent of the hearts of the Christians. Only the Master does.

John 15:20

> Remember the word that I said unto you, The servant is not greater than his lord. If they have persecuted me, they will also persecute you; if they have kept my saying, they will keep yours also.

John 15:7-8

> If ye abide in me, and my words abide in you, ye shall ask what ye will, and it shall be done unto you. Herein is my Father glorified, that ye bear much fruit; so shall ye be my disciples.

If the words dwell in us, He commands that we ask immediately what our hearts desire.

In bearing fruit, we can and will become His disciples (His followers).

The Blood Speaks

Genesis 4:10

> And he said, What hast thou done? the voice of thy brother's blood crieth unto me from the ground.

The life of Abel's blood did not cease after his murder, but cried out for vengeance. God is telling us that innocent shed blood cries out to Him for vengeance.

Hebrews 12:24

> And to Jesus the mediator of the new covenant, and to the blood of sprinkling, that speaketh better things than that of Abel.

The writer refers to the Blood of Jesus by contrasting it with Abel's blood and calling it "the blood of sprinkling, that SPEAKETH better things than that of Abel." Abel's blood cried vengeance; Jesus' Blood cried mercy.

Hebrews 9

Then verily the first covenant had also ordinances of divine service, and a worldly sanctuary. For there was a tabernacle made; the first, wherein was the candlestick, and the table, and the shewbread; which is called the sanctuary.

And after the second veil, the tabernacle which is called the Holiest of all; Which had the golden censer, and the ark of the covenant overlaid round about with gold, wherein was the golden pot that had manna, and Aaron's rod that budded, and the tables of the covenant; And over it the cherubims of glory shadowing the mercyseat; of which we cannot now speak particularly.

Now when these things were thus ordained, the priests went always into the first tabernacle, accomplishing the service of God. But into the second went the high priest alone once every year, not without blood, which he offered for himself, and for the errors of the people: The Holy Ghost this signifying, that the way into the holiest of all was not yet made manifest, while as the first tabernacle was yet standing: Which was a figure for the time then present, in which were offered both gifts and sacrifices, that could not make him that did the service perfect, as pertaining to the conscience; Which stood only in meats and drinks, and divers washings, and carnal ordinances, imposed on them until the time of reformation.

But Christ being come an high priest of good things to come, by a greater and more perfect tabernacle, not made with hands, that is to say, not of this building; Neither by the blood of goats and calves, but by his own blood he entered in once into the holy place, having obtained eternal redemption for us. For if the blood of bulls and of goats, and the ashes of an heifer sprinkling the unclean, sanctifieth to the purifying of the flesh: How much more shall the blood of Christ, who through the eternal Spirit offered himself without spot to God, purge your conscience from dead works to serve the living God?

And for this cause he is the mediator of the new testament, that by means of death, for the redemption of the transgressions that were under the first testament, they which are called might receive the promise of eternal inheritance. For where a testament is, there must also of necessity be the death of the testator. For a testament is of force after men are dead: otherwise it is of no strength at all while the testator liveth. Whereupon neither the first testament was dedicated without blood. For when Moses had spoken every precept to all the people according to the law, he took the blood of calves and of goats, with water, and scarlet wool, and hyssop, and sprinkled both the book, and all the people, Saying, This is the blood of the

> testament which God hath enjoined unto you.
>
> Moreover he sprinkled with blood both the tabernacle, and all the vessels of the ministry. And almost all things are by the law purged with blood; and without shedding of blood is no remission. It was therefore necessary that the patterns of things in the heavens should be purified with these; but the heavenly things themselves with better sacrifices than these.
>
> For Christ is not entered into the holy places made with hands, which are the figures of the true; but into heaven itself, now to appear in the presence of God for us: Nor yet that he should offer himself often, as the high priest entereth into the holy place every year with blood of others; For then must he often have suffered since the foundation of the world: but now once in the end of the world hath he appeared to put away sin by the sacrifice of himself.
>
> And as it is appointed unto men once to die, but after this the judgment: So Christ was once offered to bear the sins of many; and unto them that look for him shall he appear the second time without sin unto salvation.

The result of such sprinkling was that God manifested His Shekinah glory and spoke to the Hight Priest from between the two cherubim which overshadowed the mercy seat. It is interesting to note that the glory was *seen* and the voice *heard only* when the *Blood was used.* Even so today.

From the Wings of Heaven

⁄ Notes for a Fulfilling Christian Life ⁄

Hebrews 10:20-22

> By a new and living way, which he hath consecrated for us, through the veil, that is to say, his flesh; And having an high priest over the house of God; Let us draw near with a true heart in full assurance of faith, having our hearts sprinkled from an evil conscience, and our bodies washed with pure water.

Some offer works, emotions, strange fire, and various kinds of worship. To enter into heavenly places with Christ Jesus, we can only do so as we consciously offer the Blood of Jesus as our plea.

Some offer works, emotions, strange fire, and various kinds of worship. To enter into heavenly places with Christ Jesus, we can only do so as we consciously offer the Blood of Jesus as our plea.

To plead the Blood of Jesus is to confess to God that we are depending wholly on His mercy. *When we plead the Blood of Jesus, it immediately pleads for us*, because it is SPEAKING BLOOD. It speaks mercy from the mercy seat in Heaven where Jesus is seated with His Father.

To those who have discovered the secret, the whole realm of God's power is opened, and all the angels in heaven come to help and rescue the child of God who honors, uses, and pleads the Blood of Jesus. *The Spirit answers to the Blood.*

The reason that so many Christians are feeble, sick, and fearful today is because they have not been taught to use the Blood of Jesus as a covering.

Hebrews 12:24

> And to Jesus the mediator of the new covenant, and to the blood of sprinkling, that speaketh better things than that of Abel.

We are come to the Blood of sprinkling. This is for us to do today. We must *now* battle the principalities and powers and wicked spirits of the devil; therefore we sprinkle that precious Blood once shed for us, and Satan and his demon powers must give ground. They may be stubborn, but Christians should also be stubborn. We possess the winning weapons.

We must now battle the principalities and powers and wicked spirits of the devil; therefore we sprinkle that precious Blood once shed for us, and Satan and his demon powers must give ground.

Because the enemy is stubborn, the victory does not always come easily. Sometimes we need to battle with the Blood in prayer for weeks and months. But victory is certain.

I Peter 2:5

> Ye also, as lively stones, are built up a spiritual

> house, an holy priesthood, to offer up spiritual sacrifices, acceptable to God by Jesus Christ.

We are as the priests who offered up the blood sacrifices on behalf of the people. We offer the Blood of Jesus as our plea on behalf of ourselves, our children, and our loved ones.

The destroyer gets through the Blood line if it has been *let down by disobedience.*

The New Testament makes it clear that we must sprinkle the Blood of Jesus with faith and obedience.

Ruby with her husband Edgar on their anniversary cruise to Alaska.

www.ingramcontent.com/pod-product-compliance
Lightning Source LLC
Chambersburg PA
CBHW061145040426
42445CB00013B/1559